Sharing Writing Skills

Sharing Writing Skills

Randwick Writers' Group

Dina Davis
Garth Alperstein
Susan Beinart
Helene Grover
Anne Skyvington
Geraldine Star

Sharing Writing Skills
ISBN 978 1 76041 890 8
Copyright © text Randwick Writers' Group 2020
Copyright © cover Green Avenue Design

First published 2020 by
Ginninderra Press
PO Box 3461 Port Adelaide 5015
www.ginninderrapress.com.au

Contents

Foreword	7
Introduction	9
Guidelines for Randwick Writers' Group	11
Dina Davis	13
Garth Alperstein	27
Susan Beinart	37
Helene Grover	45
Anne Skyvington	59
Geraldine Star	77
Selected Readings: Books and Writers' Blogs	85
Acknowledgements	89

We are social animals, but our creativity sometimes demands we withdraw into loneliness to write the work that only as individuals we can do. This tension between necessary solitude and our social and communal creative needs is the trigger for a writers' group, like this one, one in which we confront our common problems and share our work so that we can go into the cockpit of writing with greater courage and greater certainty. Long live the writers' group.

Thomas Keneally

Foreword

The idea for this collection of our writings arose from a wish to show how the Randwick Writers' Group has brought our writing to the next level. Throughout the pages of this book, you will see the ways our group has nurtured each of us as writers, with encouragement and feedback.

After convening the group for over five years, I suggested that we pool our ideas together to share our skills and progress with other aspiring writers.

In 2013 we held the first meeting of the group, never dreaming that we would still exist in 2019. In convening the group, I tried to find likely candidates who were serious about writing, were prepared to spend time and energy to give and receive serious feedback, and who lived locally.

Each of our members now contributes their unique strengths, which when combined achieve truly impressive results. Some specialise in grammar and punctuation (the Comma Queens), some in narrative structure, and others in setting and characterisation.

We base our feedback on the 'sandwich' analogy: the top slice is a positive response to the work, the meat in the sandwich is a more detailed look at what could be improved in the text, and the bottom slice of our sandwich is a global comment. In this way, we respect each writer's sensitivity, while giving honest feedback.

Respecting the individual's unique voice is an overriding principle. We bounce ideas off each other, with many 'Aha!' exclamations punctuating our feedback. There is rarely any competition; rather it's as if we are one body working towards the same end – validation for each of us as writers, and eventual publication of our work.

All of us have made progress, with three of our original group achieving publication. Several of our members have completed a major work through their diligence and commitment, and are now working on a second novel or memoir.

Most importantly, we have fun at our meetings, always including a delicious morning tea to keep the brain well fuelled, and time for the latest writing gossip. If one of us has attended a writers' festival or workshop, we share the most pertinent information. We also encourage each other towards publication, and share ideas about approaching the ever-evolving book industry.

Anyone can decide to set up a similar group. But be warned – the work can be demanding and time-consuming. Both the preparation of each month's excerpt, and the exacting feedback, take time and commitment. However, the rewards are manifold: first and foremost, the monthly deadline means we actually get the writing done; it is then expertly critiqued by our fellow writers, who combine energies towards perfecting our work.

We are a company of writers, proud of our work and each other. For you, our readers, we showcase excerpts that have been shaped and polished through the group's collaboration.

It has been an honour and a privilege to convene Randwick Writers' Group over the past five years.

Dina Davis
Convenor, Randwick Writers' Group

Introduction

Collaboration, communications and consideration are the touchstones of writers' groups. Being a member of a writers' group is like taking part in a gathering at a village meeting place. Your stories get their first public airing; people comment, provide feedback that you might or might not agree with; ideas are pooled; a new writing technique may be revealed; all being designed to help and inspire you. In that meeting place away from the environment of solitude where you work, gone for the moment is the gnashing of teeth and pulling of hair so often associated with the writing process.

Randwick Writers' Group has been operating for several years. Over this time we have built a 'wisdom box' that contains tips on how to share knowledge, resources and feedback in an open and respectful environment. This book communicates our journeys and thoughts, and provides samples of our writing with you, our wider audience. It represents an opportunity for you to look into how a writers' group operates, at some successes members have had, and to take away some ideas for your own writing.

Each member has approached their contribution differently.

Dina Davis has just had her first novel published, *Capriccio: A Novel*. She explains the journey of writing from childhood to becoming an author, including how important it was to reach out to others in workshops and writers' groups in order to acquire help with and inspiration for her work.

There are glimpses of how people came to write. Garth Alperstein was a reluctant writer. It took encouragement for him to articulate and publish *The Fourpenny Axe and a Snooker Cue*, his memories of growing up in the small town that the Xhosa people called eBofolo, otherwise known as Fort Beaufort, in the Eastern Cape of South Africa.

Helene Grover was hanging from the rafters at a young age – well, not – but she began writing on the walls of her home when she was four. She is the author of *Laugh Aerobics*, and now has another manuscript, *Sometimes the Music*, ready for publication. This is a memoir of her life interwoven with the jazz world and a musician partner.

Themes of loss, racism and cross-culturalism, taken from her own experience of leaving South Africa for Australia and then teaching English to migrants, influence Susan Beinart's writing. She has published and won awards for her short stories, and has two novel manuscripts, *Thin Skin* and *The Great Trek*, about to seek publication.

Anne Skyvington is another prolific award-winning writer, publishing her short stories, poems and book reviews on her blog site. In the excerpts from her novel, *Karrana*, she sets out to show that macro-level questions are important to keep in mind, as are sentence-level and chapter-length edits, when one is writing the first or second draft of a novel.

A sense of place in the Australian landscape, plus how imagination and reading propelled Geraldine Star's writing, are also explored in this book. Her excerpt from *Riding the Storm* gives a vivid description, stirred by imagination, of the mother of one of the main characters as backstory. She outlines the importance of being a member of writing groups for obtaining feedback and taking your writing to another level.

We invite you to dip in and out of this book to gain knowledge about how a writers' group operates, to see how other writers have gone about drafting their work, and to read good writing. Enjoy…

Randwick Writers' Group

Guidelines for Randwick Writers' Group

Because we want to keep numbers manageable, the group is limited to six, and membership is by invitation. Criteria for membership include the production of a major work such as a novel or memoir, and commitment to our guidelines, as follows.

We meet on the first Wednesday of the month for approximately three hours.

We rotate venues from house to house as convenient, giving us a private and friendly environment.

Excerpts with a word limit between 2,000 and 3,000 are submitted a week before the meeting. Submissions are made as hard copy or online.

Members then review each excerpt and either email detailed feedback before the meeting, or provide the feedback face to face when we meet.

Feedback is always positive, constructive and reciprocal.

If desired, and if there is time, we read aloud one or two pages of a submission.

We respect each writer's unique voice, and their right to reject feedback.

We support and encourage each other, professionally, socially and emotionally.

Dina Davis

Dina Davis lives in the Top End of Australia and on the Eastern seaboard of New South Wales. She has twice been shortlisted for the NT Literary Awards, first in 2015 for her essay, 'Capriccio: the Lost Poems of Ted Hughes', and again in 2018 for her short story, 'Edge'. Her writing has been published in several collections and anthologies.

Dina has worked as a yoga teacher, librarian, lecturer in English, equal opportunity officer and academic editor. She has an MA in English and Linguistics, a Diploma in Education, and a Diploma in Book Publishing and Editing. She has also completed courses at the Sydney Writers' Studio, the Centre for Continuing Education, Writing NSW and the Northern Territory Writers' Centre. When not writing, Dina practises yoga, attends film festivals, and studies Kabbalah. She is currently working on her second novel, working title *A Difficult Daughter*. *Capriccio: A Novel* is her début publication. More about Dina can be found at https://www.amazon.com/author/dinadavis\; https://dinadavisauthor.com

My writing journey

> Prowling about the rooms, sitting down, getting up, stirring the fire, looking out of [the] window, tearing my hair, sitting down to write, writing nothing, writing something and tearing it up, going out, coming in, a monster to my family, a dreadful phenomenon to myself.
>
> Charles Dickens

When I was eight years old, our teacher went around the class asking children the age-old question, 'What do you want to be when you grow up?' The boys said either 'a soldier' or 'a carpenter'. The girls wanted to be 'a nurse' or 'a teacher'. When it came to my turn, I stood up and said, 'I want to be an authoress, like Ethel Turner' (author of the famous Australian classic, *Seven Little Australians*). There was a momentary shocked silence, before the entire class, including the teacher, burst into loud laughter.

I hung my head and decided never to admit to such a shameful ambition again. I became a closet writer, secretly filling journals with stories, poems and memories, as well as obsessively recording my dreams. As a single mother for over twenty years, I had to put more serious writing on hold. During my working life, I produced many reports, submissions and non-fiction articles, but rarely works of the imagination which I longed to write.

After retirement from my work as a teacher, policy writer and manager of education centres, I finally achieved my dream of writing a work of fiction. After all, my children were grown and gone, my casual work as a university tutor was not demanding, and I finally had some time to write. What was stopping me? Only myself. The quotation above from the great novelist Charles Dickens says it all: I was confronted with the dreaded writer's block, 'tearing my hair' when the words wouldn't come, and losing belief in myself as a writer day by day.

I became a writers' group junkie, avidly attending every group, workshop or course that offered guidelines and advice to aspiring writers. Regardless of the archive boxes stacked full of stories, poems and journals I'd produced over almost a lifetime, I would never have described myself as a writer.

I was in the Top End of Australia in the wet season, when the monsoonal rain thunders down, obliterating not only the landscape, but also outdoor activities. What else was there to do but write? I penned a short story, 'The Ring' and entered it into a competition. To my amazement, it won. It wasn't the $100 prize that thrilled me, but the recognition from someone outside myself that I could possibly become a writer.

The idea for the Randwick Writers' Group first came to me back in 2013. Searching for the perfect group was an adventure in itself. Some were excuses for social get-togethers, others highly competitive or, in practical terms, just too far away.

I was so busy running from workshop to workshop, group to group, there was almost no time to write. Of course it was fun to meet like-minded people, learning the many theories of how to write, but something was missing. I decided to form a new writing group, of people who lived locally, and who were serious about producing written work.

Along the way, I did several short courses in the craft of writing, with such established authors as Patti Miller, Kate Grenville and Sue Woolfe, to name a few. Then, on one of my many trips to Darwin, I joined the Darwin Authors Group. There I found my model: meetings of three hours once a month, work emailed around the group before the meeting, a manageable limit of two thousand words, and feedback based on the sandwich analogy as described in my foreword: the meat of serious critiques cushioned between positive and global feedback. I wrote a lot in this group, and learned a lot. The only problem was geographical: being based in Darwin, by nature an itinerant population, the members changed from month to month. Besides, Darwin is almost four thousand kilometres away from my 'other' home in Sydney.

Thus, I decided to form my own writing group back home in Sydney's Randwick, using the model above. I found several enthusiastic local writers, all with major works in progress, who agreed to the guidelines mentioned in the Introduction.

In 2014 I attended a Master Class in Writing presented by the acclaimed Australian novelist Thomas Keneally, and the author Claire Corbett. It was there that I met Geraldine Star, and invited her to join Randwick Writers' Group. Keneally liked my early chapters of *Capriccio* and urged me to submit the novel for publication. The rest is history.

The Randwick Writers' Group is now well into its sixth year. Most of the original members have lasted the distance, while some who found the work too arduous, or had their own reasons, have moved on.

The results have been phenomenal: two out of the present group have now been published, and a former member has had several publishing successes. Members at an earlier stage of writing receive benefit from the expertise of those more advanced. Rather than competition, we practise collaboration and encouragement, plus lots of delicious morning teas for the essential gossip sessions.

Most importantly, our group is careful never to change a writer's unique voice. It is entirely up to each of us to accept or reject suggestions, remembering the submitted extract is our own work-in-progress. We, the authors, have the last word. In this way we build confidence in each other, learning to accept or reject feedback graciously.

Many decades after that first humiliation as an ambitious eight-year-old, I have finally achieved my goal: a published novel. I cannot describe the feelings of unreality, cautious pride and utter relief that overcame me when I held the first proof copy in my hands. My début work of fiction, *Capriccio: a Novel*, was published by Cilento Press in August 2018, and is receiving great reviews.

It's taken my entire life to achieve my goal of becoming an author, and I would never have made it without the support and encouragement of the Randwick Writers' Group. Its members have walked the rocky road with me every step of the way, giving honest feedback when it was needed, and picking me up on the frequent occasions I fell into the slough of despond. I can never thank my company of writers enough for keeping my spirits fuelled for the next chapter, and the next.

More about the Randwick Writers' Group can be found on the Facebook page Randwick Writers' Group, convened by Dina Davis.

❧

How feedback changed (or didn't change) this chapter

The following excerpt is from the latest draft of my novel in progress, *A Difficult Daughter*. It is the all-important first chapter. It's the story of a young girl who suffers from a mysterious illness, and is set in Australia in the nineteen fifties.

I asked my fellow writers the following questions:

Should I turn the second section (after the first asterisk) into the beginning?

Should I leave out the plane trip altogether?

Should I leave the plane trip as first section, but change from past to present tense?

Some, but not all, members of our group thought I should put the second section first. One writer suggested a small change to the first sentence. Another wanted me to leave out the plane trip altogether. One member simply wrote, 'Don't mess with it!' I accepted some, but not all suggestions. In some cases, I could see definite improvements, and gratefully accepted the feedback.

*

1

Flying over clouds that looked like peaks of snowy white meringues, Ivy remembered how her mother would drop the little white blobs onto an oven tray. Her mouth watered, imagining those blobs becoming sweet mouthfuls, tinged golden brown, still chewy on the inside, crumbly outside. *There I go, thinking about food again.*

It was the first time in her thirteen years that Ivy had been in an aeroplane. Sitting next to Daddy, she was comforted by the contrasting scent of tobacco and cologne, and something else sweet and spicy, that special Daddy smell. It lulled her to sleep when he lay beside her at night, his back turned to her. She'd snuggle her body into the curve of his back, inhaling him through the warm serge of his suit. But that was Before.

Ivy couldn't believe how lucky she was, to have Daddy all to herself. He hadn't said how long they'd be going for. Ivy hoped it would only be a week, because otherwise she'd miss the beginning of third term.

She couldn't afford to miss any more school, not after that time away in Winchester, where they'd put the wet pads on her forehead. She didn't want to think about that now; it would only spoil the holiday.

The air hostess was dressed in a navy-blue suit with gold buttons down the front. Her bottle-blonde hair was done up in what people called a French roll, although why it was called French, Ivy couldn't imagine. When Miss French Roll brought a plastic tray of food with clever little compartments for each item, it was easy for Ivy to tell Daddy she felt a bit queasy, and wasn't hungry. Daddy just sighed, and his face took on that black look, the look he got when he argued with Mum.

'Try just a little bit, Ivy. Remember, you had no breakfast.'

'I was much too excited to eat then. Besides, I read in a magazine that it's best to start a plane trip with an empty stomach, in case you get airsick. That's what these brown paper bags are for, you know. In case one of us throws up.'

Her strategy worked; Daddy stopped looking at the untasted food on her tray. He took a bread roll from its specially recessed slot on Ivy's tray, and ate it with hard chews, as if he were angry with it. Ivy moved closer to him, and rested her head on his arm. He was unusually silent, not even in the mood for one of their arguments. They weren't really fights, only talks about anything at all they could disagree about, like 'Does God exist?' And 'If not, why not?'

She wanted to talk to Daddy, to get him to smile or laugh, like he did whenever she said something especially clever. He always ended an argument by saying, 'You're a born philosopher, Ivy, just like your grandfather was, and you've got plenty of chutzpah besides.' He seemed proud of her boldness, even though she knew it sometimes verged on rudeness.

But that was Before, when life was ordinary, Before the orange juice, and the wheelchair, and the giant overcoat she'd had to wear to school. It was Before she went mad, screaming through the quiet sensible streets for her mother to come home, not knowing why, or where she was, crying and calling out senseless words. It was Before the doctor came, and talked quietly to Mum and Daddy outside her bedroom door, but not quietly enough for Ivy to catch a few words – 'sensitive', 'nervous', and the big one, 'psychological'.

The aeroplane smelled of leather and disinfectant. Daddy took a cigarette from the packet he always kept in his right trouser pocket, then dug deeper, searching for matches. The brown stain on his forefinger reminded Ivy of those mornings at the breakfast table, when he'd stabbed the air to make his point. It was so much part of Daddy, that finger. He lifted his hand and waved at the air hostess as she swung down the aisle, a fixed smile on her lipsticked mouth.

'I wonder – would you have a match, my dear?' He used that smooth voice, the one he used with Ivy's teachers, or Mum's lady friends.

Ivy knew in advance that the hostess would lean closer, and her fake smile would melt into a different one; *more like a simper*, thought Ivy.

'One moment, sir.' The hostess was looking straight into Daddy's eyes. She walked towards the front of the plane, her hips swaying.

Looking at her father, Ivy saw his eyes behind their horn-rimmed spectacles follow the hostess's wiggling backside. She walked slowly towards them, holding a silver lighter.

Daddy was holding the unlit cigarette between his fingers. The hostess leaned over Daddy, and held the lighter to his cigarette. Ivy could smell her scent; it was sickeningly sweet, and made her draw back.

Daddy leaned forward, his hand almost touching the hostess's crimson fingernails. 'Allow me,' he said in his faint English accent, gently taking the lighter from the hostess, snapping it open, and looking deeply into her eyes. The red-gold flame flared between them in the moment before he touched it to the tip of his cigarette. 'Thank you, my dear.' Daddy's voice was smooth as honey.

Ivy noticed a red flush creeping up the hostess's neck as she straightened, the smile on her face fixed again. 'My pleasure,' she said.

*

Ivy had fallen asleep on her father's shoulder. In her dream, she was back in Winchester. Margaret, the woman she'd befriended in the hospital, was jerking like a puppet gone haywire. Ivy sat up straight, and shook her auburn curls to get the ghastly dream out of her head. The plane gave a sudden jolt, and a baby started to cry.

'Will we get off in Adelaide?' she asked her father sleepily.

'We have an hour at the airport, time to get a bite to eat, something better than this aeroplane slop. Don't blame you for leaving it, Ivy. You must be hungry.'

Of course she was hungry. Starving to death, literally. She'd perfected the art of not eating, obeying the voice in her head that was far, far stronger than the hunger that gnawed at her belly.

'I'm OK, better not eat just in case I might have to use one of those airsick bags.'

Daddy patted her hand, not looking at her. His expression was sad, and angry too. She knew what he was thinking, and wanted more than anything to make him smile again, and to laugh with her again.

The plane landed with a series of bumps. The baby, probably shocked into silence, stopped crying. People were unclicking their seatbelts, standing up and stretching.

The air hostess stood in the aisle, and announced, 'Good evening, and thank you for flying with Trans Australia Airlines. We have landed in Adelaide, where the time is six-twenty p.m. It's a balmy seventy-three degrees outside. Would all passengers take their hand luggage with them off the plane while it is being cleaned and fumigated for your comfort. We will be taking off for Perth at seven-thirty p.m. Please enjoy the facilities of Adelaide airport.'

Ivy was relieved that there was no further eye contact between Daddy and the air hostess. Following him down the steel steps and across the dusty tarmac, she clutched her schoolbag, which she'd packed with enough books for a week or two.

The airport had a desolate air, as if it knew no one wanted to be there. To Daddy's disgust and Ivy's relief, there was no hot food, except for pre-packed ham and tomato sandwiches on thick white bread.

'Not kosher,' muttered Daddy.

'Too bad,' sighed Ivy.

They sat on some rickety metal chairs. Daddy lit another cigarette, and Ivy took out her Latin homework.

'Listen to me, *Ivy*. When we get to Perth, I want you to make a good impression. Especially on your Uncle Sid and Aunt Sonia. Don't hide away with your books all the time, they won't like that. And remember the names of your cousins, Alex and Deborah.'

Daddy had used the diminutive of her name, which he only ever did when there was something serious to say. Ivy closed her Latin primer with a sigh, the comforting words *amo, amas, amat* fading from her sight.

'How old are they?'

'I wouldn't know, my dear. It's your mother who keeps track of these things. Younger than you, all of them, I'd say. The little one's only a baby.'

*

The first thing Ivy noticed when they landed in Perth was the space. It was as if the city were an empty house, waiting to be furnished. Houses she saw through the taxi's window were few and far between, with flat roofs, squatting like mushrooms higgledy-piggledy in a field. Not like the crowded streets of Sydney back home.

Daddy, sitting close beside her on the sticky leather seat of the taxicab, lit another cigarette. Neither of them spoke, exhausted by the long flight. Ivy breathed in his acrid smoke, grateful for its familiar smell. She was starting to feel queasy, her stomach clenching more in fear than in hunger. She'd managed to eat nothing so far except the barley sugar sweet she was given to suck by the smiley hostess, which was supposed to stop the earache you got as the plane made its descent.

The taxi pulled up outside a large sprawling house, with a red light illuminating a sign over the front porch: Dr S Bronsky, General Practitioner. Hours: 8 a.m. to 1 p.m. Monday to Friday, 3 p.m. to 7 p.m.

Monday to Thursday. There was a phone number underneath, and a note in small writing: *House Calls Available After Hours.*

Ivy was impressed, and so, obviously, was her father, who pointed at the sign and said to the taxi driver, a young man hardly out of his teens, 'My brother-in-law, you know. Put himself through medicine by working in a fruit shop. You have to give him credit…'

'Dr Bronsky's a household word round here, mate. He brought me and my brother into the world, and saw my grandma out of it. Wouldn't go to anyone else.'

Ivy saw Daddy's smile of satisfaction, as he handed the boy a crisp pound note.

'Keep the change, son,' he said.

The boy looked wide-eyed at the money in his hand and quickly pocketed it. He sprang from the cab to open the boot. That was when Ivy noticed her father had brought his small pigskin bag, not the big suitcase that stood in the hall back home, the one with the thick strap around it to help it close against its bulging contents. She felt relieved. Only a week.

Her own suitcase was new, containing more books, as well as the clothes Mum had helped her pack. Far too many for a week. 'Winter ones as well as summer,' her mother had said, 'because the weather's so changeable in Perth, Ivy. You might need your jumpers, as well as some summer dresses, and I've packed one good skirt to wear on Friday nights, and a good dress for Shule. It's too big for you now, but we're not wasting money on new clothes. Please God you'll fill out again soon, so these'll fit you again.'

It was still early morning, the air fresh and crisp, as Ivy and Daddy stood on the front porch of 30 Claremont Highway, waiting for an answer to Daddy's firm knock. The silence hung between them.

After several long minutes, a tall thin woman with red hair arranged in carefully crimped waves, opened the heavy front door. 'Doctor's not open yet,' she said crossly.

'That's all right, my dear,' said Daddy. 'I'm Sid's brother-in-law, and this is my daughter, Ivy. You can call me Abe. And what might your name be, pretty girl like you, eh?'

Ivy noticed two red patches flaring on her cheeks. She stared in fascination as the patches spread over the woman's face.

'Oh, sorry, Mister. Me name's Daphne. I'm Dr Bronsky's secretary. I s'pose you'd better come in then. This door's only for patients, just so's you know. Family comes in round the side.'

They followed the girl into a dark room set about with several high-backed chairs. There was a small table in the middle, piled with *Women's Weekly*s, some tattered, their once bright covers dull.

'The waiting room,' Daphne announced.

As if we couldn't see for ourselves, Ivy said to herself.

Daphne used a key from the bunch at her waist to open a door leading into a dimly lit living room. There was a sofa covered in purplish brocade, and some easy chairs.

'Sit y'selves down,' said Daphne. 'I'll get Mrs Bronsky.'

'Can I read those magazines, Miss Daphne?'

'It's just Daphne to you, young lady. Course you can. They're a bit old, but. I'll be bringing new ones when me mum's finished with them.'

Ivy perched on the edge of a large chair, its seat sagging sadly. She thought it might not bear even her weight. She took a *Women's Weekly* and turned its yellowing pages. It was full of advertisements for the new shiny refrigerators, which people were buying to replace the old ice chests.

Daddy sat across from her on the sofa, his long trousered legs crossed. He seemed to be appraising the room, with a look of disapproval. 'Not what you're used to at home, eh? Needs a good coat of paint and some new furniture, I'd say.'

Before Ivy could respond, she felt someone watching her. Turning, she saw a little boy of about six, his dark eyes staring at her under floppy brown hair.

'Hello. You must be Alexander,' she said, relieved to see a sign of life in this silent house. 'I'm your cousin Ivy from Sydney.'

There was a gap where his front tooth should be, which Ivy thought made him endearing. He was still wearing his pyjamas.

'It's Alex for short,' the boy said, with a slight lisp. A moment's hesitation, then he was off.

A cough sounded from the hallway, and a short round woman, her housecoat flapping open, rushed into the room. 'Abe,' she cried in a phlegmy voice, 'is it here you are already? Such *nachas*!' Ivy knew she meant 'such a pleasure'. It sounded rude in Yiddish. 'How is it you did get here? Don't tell me you *schlepped* all the way from the airport on the bus? My Sid, he wanted to pick you up, even so busy he is.' There was reproach in her voice, which rose sharply with each question.

Daddy got to his feet and crossed the room, to embrace his sister-in-law, as she hastily tied the sash of her housecoat around her waist. 'So good to see you, Sonia. Lily sends her love, of course. We're both so grateful for this.'

Ivy wondered what it was Daddy was so grateful for: was it the offer of a lift not taken? A seat on a lumpy sofa? But her thoughts were stopped by a strident cry from Aunt Sonia. She stared with a look of horror at Ivy, who sent a silent thought message to Daddy: let's not stay here, let's get a hotel, let's go home tomorrow, but he was smiling the smile he kept for visitors, and grasping Aunt Sonia's chubby hands.

'So this is your Ivy? *Oy gewalt*, now I see what you mean by your letters. All skins and bone, she is. Ha! Just wait for Sonia's special *cholent* and cheesecake. For sure it will make her fatter.'

'You mustn't worry yourself, Sonia. You have enough to do, with feeding your own brood. Ivy's a big girl now, thirteen already, she can look after herself. And be a help to you, too.'

'A help? She looks like she cannot lift even an envelope. Come here, girlie, let me to look at you.'

Ivy stood up and walked slowly towards her aunt. Face to face, she saw darting black eyes, sharp cheekbones, strangely flared nostrils. It made Ivy think there must be a bad smell, and maybe it was herself? Unwashed after the long journey?

But when Aunt Sonia drew breath to talk, her nostrils stayed wide. 'Just look at you, girl! How could you do such a thing to your so good parents? There'll be no nonsense in this house, you know.'

Ivy stared back at her aunt. 'You're not my aunt really, only by marriage, and that doesn't count.' The words rushed out of Ivy's mouth before she could stop them. Her fists clenched inside the too-long sleeves of her cardigan, which she'd pulled down to warm her hands.

'Of course Sonia's your aunt. Apologise immediately! I'm so sorry, Sonia, my Ivy gets carried away sometimes, and forgets her manners.'

Ivy glimpsed the shadow of a smile behind Daddy's moustache.

Garth Alperstein

From a reluctant writer to publication

I have never seen myself as a writer, but my wife convinced me that I had a story to tell, if for nobody else but our children.

I am a semi-retired paediatrician with a specialty in child and youth public health. I have published in excess of seventy publications in medical literature, but this was my first publication in the genre of creative writing.

I was born in 1950 in a small town in the Eastern Cape, South Africa, to a Jewish family who had fled the pogroms in Russia and Eastern Europe at the end of the nineteenth century. The town was started as a military outpost by the British colonial government in 1822 and was named Fort Beaufort. The Xhosa people of the area called it eBofolo. My wife, Melissa, grew up in suburban Port Elizabeth, the fifth largest town in South Africa.

When we met in 1970, I would tell her stories about characters and events that I recalled from my childhood. She found these stories incredible and encouraged me to write them down. I ignored her pleas and encouragements for many years, until two events finally motivated me to start to put fingers to keyboard. In April 1994, my parents' pub, Deane's Commercial Hotel, burned down, and within a month Nelson Mandela was elected president of South Africa. These events, an end of an era for my family, and the beginning of a new era for the country, occurring almost simultaneously, were too symbolic for me to ignore any longer, and I started to write.

Initially, since I was working full time, I wrote only during holidays. I also elected to do an evening course on creative writing at Sydney City

East Community College. The teacher running the course started the first session by saying, 'If you want to write, there are two things you have to do – read, read, read, and read, and write, write, write and write. There are no short cuts.'

Not being a big reader of novels, I thought to myself, 'I don't read much, but I can write!' Over time, I discovered how wrong I was and how right she was. Along the way, two friends, Ian David and Smoky Robinson, who were writers, also gave me feedback, and suggestions for the structure of the story. Each time, that resulted in more writing, more structural change, and more drafts, each one a little better than the previous version.

A friend informed me about the Bondi Writers' Group, which met on a Sunday afternoon once a month and where I came into contact with other writers who provided me with very helpful feedback on my writing.

However, I didn't become really productive until I mostly retired from full-time work and was fortunate enough to be invited by Dina Davis to join the Randwick Writers' Group. We met every fortnight. I learned not only from receiving constructive feedback from the group on my story, but also by having to provide constructive feedback to the others in the group. The group reviewed every chapter of my book over a year, providing invaluable feedback and suggestions for improvement. Having not been a very good English scholar at school, I was particularly grateful for their grammatical input. My book turned out to be mostly a memoir, but with some fictionalised history woven through the memoir. Most of the group, and others whose opinion I had sought, had recommended against combining the two genres. However, I was determined to write the book as such, and they graciously assisted me to combine the two. I also enjoyed the camaraderie of the group, and delicious morning tea halfway through our sessions.

Finally, I was very fortunate to have had my book published by Ginninderra Press in Port Adelaide in 2015.

Following are a few excerpts from my book *The Fourpenny Axe and a Snooker Cue: eBofolo remembered*.

*

1

Of burnt-out buildings
Many stories to tell
Lost in smoke

It is 1996. I look at the remnants of Deane's Commercial Hotel in Fort Beaufort, South Africa. The brick and cement shell of the building is still intact and the upstairs balcony still visible, but the roof is gone. The building has obvious fire damage with soot on the walls. Doors and windows are boarded up. The liquor store, called the 'Off Sales', attached to the hotel, is now a small clothes shop. Xhosa and 'coloured' women and men crowd the streets and footpaths, some selling goods on colourful mats. Unlike the Fort Beaufort of my childhood, I see few 'white' people.

Across the street the Town Hall clock is stuck on twenty-to-two. Next to the Town Hall the park is overgrown with grass and bushes. Litter clings to the maze of elephant grass hedges. My brother Neil, my sister Melanie and I stand in front of our burnt-down memory. It is a sultry, overcast day.

'Excuse me, would you please take a photograph of us in front of this building?' requests Neil of a young Xhosa woman.

Hesitantly, she takes my brother's camera from his hand, looking perplexed. Through the lens she focuses her gaze on the three people, two men and a woman, standing in front of the ruin of the hotel. In an awkward silence the wind rustles plastic bags littering the street. A few yards away, a stray dog nonchalantly chews on chicken bones in the gutter.

The woman steadies the camera and presses the button.

*

On a summer's day in 1816, Reverend Joseph Williams of the London Missionary Society stands outside his newly established mission station near the Kat River. He can hear in the distance the Hadeda Ibis making its characteristic har-dee-dar call. His main purpose is to convert Chief Maqoma and his tribe to Christianity. But this is not the beginning of Fort Beaufort.

In the distance, he sees a number of people approaching on horseback. He recognises the person leading the group. It is his dear friend Lord Charles Somerset, Governor of the Cape Province. The group arrives and dismounts.

'Lord Somerset, to what do I owe this honour?'

'Good day to you, Reverend.'

'Do come in for a cup of tea, sir, and please invite your men as well.'

The two men enter the building, followed closely by Somerset's entourage. They sit at a large wooden table covered with a tartan tablecloth. The room is small and dark, with light entering two windows on the north side. A few minutes later, a young African woman enters with a china teapot and tea cups on a silver tray, and places it on the table. She is wearing a black cloth headdress, beaded necklaces, beaded bracelets and anklets, but is otherwise scantily clothed. Lord Somerset's men, being conscious of the Reverend in the room, try not to look at her directly.

'Enkosi – thank you, Nomondi,' says Reverend Williams.

She pours the tea and leaves the room.

'Reverend, as you are aware, I have met with Chief Maqoma on a number of occasions to negotiate the cessation of cattle theft from the white farmers,' says Lord Somerset. He frowns. 'He clearly has no intention of complying with my requests. I am now forced to take action. I will order Colonel Maurice Scott to establish a military post three miles from here on the other side of the Kat River.'

'Yes, of course, Sir. I look forward to a cordial relationship with Colonel Scott.'

Lord Somerset leaves, with his men following, all turning their heads to peer through the kitchen window as they return to their horses.

*

Six years later, Colonel Maurice Scott of the Royal Warwickshire Regiment stands proudly in front of a rectangular stone building on top of the hill. After a long hot summer, the earth is parched. A warm wind stirs up swirls of dust that move swiftly across the ground then fade away as fast as they appear. Colonel Scott is dressed in his full military regalia. Before him is a small platoon of soldiers, wearing red-and-black uniforms. He twirls both sides of his moustache and clears his throat. As if on cue, the soldiers become silent.

'Men,' he announces, 'the Blockhouse is now complete. We will have a strong fortress here against the raids by the Xhosa Chief, Jongumsobomvu Maqoma. We are now very well strategically placed, as we are almost surrounded by the Kat and Brak Rivers in a horseshoe shape.' Scott stops and stares at his men with unusual intensity before adding, 'Except to the north.' Pointing now with his cane at the map set up on the makeshift table before him, he raps his cane on the area of the map where the rivers run and announces, 'Soon we will be in total control of the region when we build a couple of bridges across them.' He pauses. He looks up towards the sky, as if he is going to address the heavens. 'And now, in the name of Lord Charles Somerset, and in honour of his father, the Duke of Beaufort, I name this settlement Fort Beaufort.'

His platoon of soldiers, staring straight ahead, present arms.

In the distance, in the shadow of a mimosa thorn tree, only the whites of the eyes of a black man can be seen.

*

12

> The love of a mother
> And a surrogate child
> It's not black and white

Beauty Baardman was my other mother. She nurtured me probably more than did my own mother. Beauty was a Xhosa woman. But with a surname like Baardman, she may have married a man of Khoikhoi descent. The Khoikhoi descendants more often adopted Afrikaner surnames, assigned to them while working for Afrikaner farmers. The Xhosas often adopted English first names, in addition to their Xhosa first names, but kept their Xhosa surnames.

*

School holidays are over. I get my little brown satchel with my schoolbooks and put it on my back.

Beauty stomps into our bedroom. 'Let us bugga off!'

Beauty takes my hand and we walk to school across Campbell Street, past the War Memorial and Fort Beaufort museum, which we often visit to look at old guns, assegais and soldiers' uniforms, and down the hill to the Convent of the Sacred Heart on Durban Street. The Savoy hotel is diagonally opposite the Convent.

I look forward to the last school bell of the day because I know Beauty will be back to take me home, and will say again, 'OK, let us bugga off!'

The next morning, I wake up with small itchy blisters on my face and my chest.

'Oh shit, you have chickenpox,' says my mom, looking at my blisters. 'Let's put some calamine lotion on. That will help the itch.'

Soon after, Beauty arrives. 'What's thet rubbish on yoh face, Toto?'

'It's calamine lotion. I have chickenpox. The Madam says I can't go to school today.'

'If you want to get rid of the chickenpox, we have to go outside and dig a hole in the ground and you must say, "Huh, huh, *qiligwena*" into the hole. That will chase away the chickenpox and send it to the rich man's cattle.'

'But, Beauty, the Madam said I have to stay in bed. I'm not allowed to go outside.'

'We will have to make a hole in the room then.'

Beauty leaves the room and comes back a few minutes later with a big screwdriver. She goes to the corner of the room and with the screwdriver lifts up a piece of floorboard.

'OK. Get out of bed and shout into the hole huh, huh, *qiligwena*, huh, huh, *qiligwena*.'

I jump out of bed and shout as loud as I can, 'Huh, huh, *qiligwena*, huh, huh, *qiligwena*, huh, huh, *qiligwena*.'

'OK, *lungile*, that's enough.'

Within a few days, my chickenpox becomes all scabs, and within a week I am better. I wonder whose cattle got chickenpox. I hope it is Bull Knott's cattle because he won't let us go paling – eel-fishing – on his farm, and I know he is very rich. My dad says so.

*

I think of Beauty's concept of disease and how superstitions, myths and beliefs have influenced illness and health of all cultures. I am reading a book on the San, *The Broken String: The Last Words of an Extinct People*, which has many stories of San myths and legends.

*

On an autumn day, in about 3000 BCE, finally all is quiet and the night is nearly over. A faint light begins to appear on the horizon. A young San mother is sitting cross-legged on the ground on a hill, surrounded by river except to the north, with her baby cradled in her arm and breastfeeding. Her husband is squatting next to them quietly with his bow and kudu-hide satchel of arrows by his side. Her mother is tending to the fire.

'If you see a shooting star falling in the sky, you must squeeze the milk out of your breasts and not feed it to your baby,' says her mother earnestly. 'If the baby drinks that milk a breath of fire from the star will burn a mark on her heart. The sparks coming off the falling star are the star's lice and they can kill your baby's heart.'

The sky is clear and filled with stars.

*

42

The old San woman knows what is happening. She knows she is getting closer to the ancestors of her people. She knows her mind is here and then it is there. She hears the children's voices. The voices fade into the distance. Her vision becomes blurred, then clear, then blurred again.

The time has come. She knows what she has to do. In the distance, she sees a young girl playing in a puddle of water after a big rain. It is her. She smiles. Her eyes close slightly as a series of events race through her head. Like a moving picture, she envisions the first time she kisses her husband and he touches her breast, then suddenly she is giving birth to her first child. She stands near the big aloe tree. The pain is intense, but like her mother and her mother before her had done, she knows how to bear the pain and be silent, before her baby slides down between her legs in a gush of yellow fluid and blood. She has not known such joy, such happiness, such love. Her children run before her eyes one after the other, through their ages and stages into adulthood and then her grandchildren appear before her.

Her husband comes back from a hunt with his bow and pack of arrows over one shoulder and a deer over the other; then another one and another one. Then she sees him on the ground, shaking and shivering, turning paler by the day. He develops a rash all over his body. He can neither stand nor move. She starts to feel sad. They all know. Now she knows.

The sun is falling below the sky past the baobab tree. The horizon turns bright red, almost luminous. She picks up her two sticks. She pulls herself to a standing position and slowly, one painful step at a time, makes her way past the sleeping shelters, past the mimosa thorn trees and walks and walks until she is deep into the night and can stagger no more.

She lies down on the cold earth, clutches her sticks close to herself and looks at all the stars in the sky for the last time. She closes her eyes. There is darkness. There is silence. The wind blows away her footprints.

Susan Beinart

Honing my writing

How did I get to Randwick Writers? Geography and writing led me here five years ago. I have a long history of mixing the two.

After moving continents twice, I landed up in Sydney, then Albury, where country life inspired me to write. A constant theme, triggered by my own story, was loss. Others were racism, evoked by my South African roots, and cross-culturalism, reinforced by teaching English to migrants. In Albury, I published short stories and articles. I also contributed to a progressive novel, *Murray Time* (Latao Press, 2003), and some of my short stories won awards, including the Joseph Furphy Commemorative Literary Prize.

Back in Sydney, I completed a Graduate Diploma in Creative Writing at UTS. I also finished the second draft of *The Great Trek of the Greenhorns,* which embraces my favourite themes. It tells the stories of three families who are unprepared for their migrant lives. A later draft of my second novel, *Thin Skin*, follows the same families years later. *Thin Skin* has earned two residencies at Varuna and has won a Booranga Writers' Centre mentorship.

During my journeying and writing, I have participated in many writers' groups. Through my membership of Bondi Writers (now Waverley Writers), which has its home in Waverley Library, I re-met Dina Davis, who invited me to join Randwick Writers, then in its infancy. This would be a group, I was told, in which detailed feedback would occur.

Randwick Writers is certainly that kind of group. I cannot emphasise enough how satisfying it is. Firstly, it is a safe place in which we all look out for each other. Secondly, our members have diverse skills and experiences, which serve multiple aspects of our writing.

Unlike me, half of our current members are Australian-born, which means that I can check up on cultural and vocabulary aspects of my stories with them. For example, I have struggled with living room (South African) and lounge room (colloquial Australian) within my two novels, and also in one of my short stories in progress, 'What's Love Got to Do with It?' Set in rural Australia in the 1980s, this short story has profited too from the fact that two of our members have shared their deep cultural knowledge about Australian country life with me.

Randwick Writers has also influenced the excerpts from *Thin Skin* that I have included in this collection. In particular, the group has helped me to focus on words and sentences. I have followed their feedback by editing out unnecessary words and adding clarifying ones, and as a result my sentences have become crisper. For example, my first chapter has become more like the hook it is meant to be, to entice readers to read on.

I am still sharing *Thin Skin* with Randwick Writers, who are supplying valuable feedback as well as encouraging me to publish it. Any publishing journey, while always daunting, would be vastly more so without their support.

∽

Following are excerpts from the first and twenty-sixth chapters of *Thin Skin*.

*

Leon

One, two, three, he's in Mum's house. Three, four, five, he's up the stairs. He's about to barge into her bedroom. He opens her door and there's a sight he's never seen: Mum, a dark-skinned bloke and a turned-on lamp. In her tousled room, sprawled out together on her bed. He gasps cause he's twenty and too old to cry. Their eyes look huge; his throat's dry. He tramps back to the landing when they sit up. He's ready to run before Mum leaps off the bed.

She chucks on her gown and says, 'Leon, you're LATE.'

He sprints down the stairs, Mum trailing him. His sister Lisa follows from her room. Mum's bed-bloke, a lighter shade of Mr Mandela, isn't far behind. Now they're all four of them in a conga line. It's like, run, run as fast as you can, when everyone hot-tails poor doomed gingerbread man down to a river where a fox waits.

Downstairs, his pulse goes ninety ks per hour. Mum and Lisa sit at the round table while the dark stranger leans against the kitchen arch. This new bloke must be Mum's boyfriend – what a crappy way for him to find out. But now the loud clock ticks. It's three a.m. and he's just bolted, coughing, from a fire.

Will Mum believe what he's been through – smouldering snapshots, embers of a past now gone? He's blurting it out in the kitchen, but she won't hear. She lets him down. Lisa also shakes her head. Are the flames still forking, or is the back room he fled turning to dust?

Now his eyes start straying to Mum's grey cheeks. Has more drama been landing on her and his sister while he's lived away, sketching, these last six doped-out months?

He can't recall all the stuff Mum sticks in her big red notebook and shoves in his face till he's forced to look. But a cutting he remembers is about Meltdown Man. 'You're just like Meltdown Man,' she'd once said, 'that athlete who didn't drink enough water.' Tonight, she says it again. This time, she goes on about it. It's in her imagination – he's not like that runner at all.

'You'll win your own race in the end, just like he did,' she calls to him when he's given up and is on his way back upstairs.

Has he seen her with a man before? He's thinking this cause he's stopped craving to speak to her and is lying in his old bed. Does he want her to feel sorry she's not taking his fire seriously – is that why he mightn't speak to her any more? But, like real Meltdown Man, his pain's bigger than that. The more he lies here, the more he aches, his pathetic portrait of Mr Mandela haunting him. Like Hamlet, Prince of Denmark, he might choose real death next time.

He tries not to think of his sister, who hates him – is Lisa unlocking the drawer in her bedroom now? What family secrets has she got locked up in there – is there stuff about their dead dad? When Lisa talks about Dad, it's always about Dad and her, and about what they did together before he, Leon, was born.

Through the floorboards, he can hear the vibes doofing – is Mum still sitting and yapping about that Aussie runner who nearly died?

*

In the second excerpt, Leon and Lisa are travelling in Lisa's car, about to visit their estranged stepmother, Ruthie. Again, we witness the scene through Leon's troubled eyes.

Leon

When they reach the house where Dad used to live, Leon's got burger grease on his lips. Before and after their food stop, Lisa wowed him. She's always been narrow-minded, conservative, judgemental. Gee, that's harsh: he'll add generous to that tally. Yet he dug sitting in her car. She kept saying everything was okay, even when he spilled sauce on the seat. She told him more sad stuff about Ruthie and stopped to let him smoke on the way. He puffed on the kerb next to the car and pictured Ruthie's sharp black eyes.

He pushes open Ruthie's gate, which he doesn't kick this time, and some memories twist through him. There's that room where his small self slept a few times, an enclosed veranda Ruthie called the porch, which hangs over the spiky front garden. He used to gaze down at dark plants whenever he stayed over and couldn't sleep, striking matches to light his way to the window. Even in those days he kept matchboxes in his pockets. There's also a hidden cupboard under the stairs with a trapdoor leading to the garage. He used to hide in that space whenever his insides tightened.

Ruthie drove home from the refuge one Christmas Eve, her ringed hands empty. He was waiting with Dad, expecting a wrapped present. There weren't enough gifts under their tree, Ruthie told Dad. Leon shouldn't have expected anything. She kept on at Dad about those neglected women at the refuge, and ignored him. She knew all about how those places should run. No one else, she said in her powerful voice, knew anything. Locking her arms around his dad while his small self watched them.

When Ruthie kissed his dad's mouth, him, he ran to the hidden cupboard and kneeled on the trapdoor, his hands empty at his sides. He exploded in a sob, slid his matchbox out of his pocket and lit match after match. The trapdoor lid took ages to ignite. Dad kept calling him but a long time passed before, stiff as a bat, he fled his smoky cave-refuge. Ruthie's stare stabbed while Dad, who yelled at him, easily killed that small fire.

Back at home, he told Mum he was sorry and she bought him an electric train set he wanted that made a whistling noise he couldn't get used to. Whenever Ruthie even glanced at him after that night, he ignored her. He never allowed her to enter his world again. Mum carried on suffocating him and he kept on letting her.

Him and Lisa have walked through Ruthie's gate by now, past her greens, browns and ochres. How would it be to watch them burn?

'They're a dull lot of flora,' Lisa says, breaking into his warped enjoyment. She presses Ruthie's bell, which clangs at them.

Ruthie's shoes clatter. He knows they're hers cause her heels used to fire bullets at floorboards. She opens the door and her blonde hair tips pop out.

Whenever he knocked on her door in the old days, one of her

haunted-looking housekeepers opened it. Different women worked for her at various times. He wanted to cry when he saw them sweep or dust cause it seemed like each woman's pain matched his. He never got to know them cause he came so rarely and they'd disappear in the evenings. They had to return to their children, Dad once explained.

In her car, Lisa had told him Ruthie used to recruit staff from among the battlers at the refuge. They became her servants in a typically gross way, Lisa had said.

Ruthie stares at them. The corners of her eyes glisten like she's been crying. 'My God, look at you. All grown-up, both of you. Beautiful Lisa and fiery Leon.'

Ruthie's just the same 'cept for a thicker waist and more rings on her fingers. Her boobs look flat behind the loose purple blouse she's wearing. When she lands a kiss on him, her musky perfume reeks and bangles feel hard. Still, it's not as bad as it might have been. He watches as she grabs Lisa and lunges at her cheek. He can't believe he once feared this warm, maybe needy, woman.

Helene Grover

How it began for me

Engrossed, typing on her laptop, an auburn-haired woman was perched at a bench top behind me. I was sitting in front of her at a footpath table of the same café, also deeply involved with my laptop, busy with my new novel. I had never written sexy material before and was letting my imagination run a little wild. I looked around; it certainly wasn't for inspiration. After all, it was most unlikely anyone was going to provide me with footpath action content for my book. The woman behind me looked up and we asked each other whether we were writing a novel. That's how I first met Dina Davis, who ultimately invited me to join the Randwick Writers' Group.

There was no way of knowing how incredibly valuable this group of exceptionally creative women would be. I soon found out. Each person contributed a great deal to the progress of my writing, such as pointing out my problems with punctuation, full stops, commas and run-on sentences. Of course, I took their advice and it is to my advantage.

I started writing as a toddler. I scribbled on the walls of my parents' Paris home. There was no washable paint in those days and they had a hell of a job washing off my childish inspirations.

My passion for reading propelled me to write. I filled endless diaries with words about my growing pains as an overactive, imaginative teenager. Pad and paper are always in my handbags and pockets. No matter where I go or what I do, I write; Paris, London, Israel, the United States and aboard cruise ships. Some of those scribbles do end up in print, someplace or other.

When I was sixteen, I discovered a ladder. The hallway acoustics echoed beautifully in our little home in Erskineville. Perched up there, I composed songs, and my hit song 'Barefoot Boy' was born. Harper Collins published my book *Laugh Aerobics*, which was also translated into Japanese. I also wrote articles for newspapers and magazines. My cupboard is full of folders filled with songs and stories, and for a very long time, I believed that I wrote 'real good like'.

With the unbelievable popularity of *50 Shades of Grey*, I decided to have a go at a funny sexy novel and wrote *In Bed with Millie*. It was during this process that I discovered what editing was all about, and how vital it is towards the construct of a well-written novel.

By this stage, I had put together a structure and idea for a memoir about my twenty-six-year relationship with my alcoholic jazz musician partner, and the vagaries of our entertainment lifestyles. The author Arnold Zable convinced me that this was a better choice of book to concentrate on, and to put aside the bed stories. Of course, I took his advice.

I feel that the monthly sharing with the Randwick Writers' Group has improved my writing. I am excited to share the progress of the others' books and hope that my input is just as valuable to them as theirs is to me. What I love about the group is the support and generosity towards each other's work. I hope that this book will give other people insight into the value of a constructive writer's group. I feel that I now belong to a writer's fraternity where we are in pursuit of achieving our writing goals and ultimate publication.

Workings of the group

I don't know how other writing groups operate. In our group, what helps us all tremendously is the monthly input from each other. One week before our monthly meeting, we email each other a portion of our current book writing, around three thousand words each. This gives each one of us time to read the piece and make helpful comments when we get together for a set two hours, being respectful of the allocated time for each member.

Group members give feedback in different ways. One person sends her comments in Word Tracking which shows the exact parts that need to be improved. Another member highlights the areas of my chapter that need attention in colour. Another participant prefers to use a paper copy and brings a printed copy to our meetings.

> and sometimes it was said in jest, "it's there okay?" I would lamely reply, "Don't be silly, I'm giving you a happy-to-see-you hug."
> At one time we were going to a Great Synagogue dinner, and just when we were about to walk through the security frame he quickly turned on his heels saying, "I'll be back soon, I forgot something in the car."
> When he returned, he whispered, "I had to take my gun back to the car." I could only imagine how it would have been, had he walked through and the alarm had gone off, security guards frisking, the Rabbi praying, and the startled congregation wondering if he was Jewish.
> The gun didn't always travel in his pocket. He had left it in his music satchel in my house. When I discovered it, I asked a couple of my visiting gay friends to try and get the bullets out. They had no idea, pointing the gun into the garden, one of them fiddled about with it and luckily nothing happened. I hate to imagine a worse case scenario.
> When Serge reconnected with his gun, he realized that it had been tampered with, "Who was the idiot that released the safety catch? Did you?"
> "No, a worried friend did."
> "How dare you let them do that, you could have killed yourselves," he yelled.

Together with our practical suggestions, we also include an overall comment about the piece, whether needing major changes or just a few punctuation tweaks; I need a lot of them! The comments are always helpful, encouraging and never nasty.

As a result of these regular meetings over the last two to three years, I have learnt and improved my manuscript exponentially. I am now much more aware of how I can improve my writing. This gives me better confidence towards publishing my creative endeavour.

There are other aspects to our writing group. We also share useful information about events and contacts that can help us further. For example, an upcoming writing seminar, internet programs that can be useful, and currently for me, contacts for an independent publishing company, who are currently working with me to publish my manuscript. The company, Cilento Press, includes copy editing, cover design, layout and uploads, as well as hard copies of my book, *Sometimes the Music*. After chasing a multitude of very costly overseas companies for this service, it's a joy to be able to pick up the phone and discuss with this helpful publishing team all facets of my publishing process.

&

Following are two chapters from *Sometimes the Music*.

*

1 – Playing with Memory

> Life is a lot like jazz – it's best when you improvise
> George Gershwin

Silence brought me memories, and music made them dance.

I clutched my doll to my chest and dived through the partially open French window. Glass shattered into the room and a large piece tore into my father's leg. The gash on my arm opened an exit for the blood to stream down my skin.

Seconds before, I played quietly outside on an extended rooftop while my father read his daily paper.

The man upstairs dangled a piece of string down from his window and threatened me, 'I'm going to get your dolly.'

I was five years old and believed him, which led to my frantic escape to rescue my favourite toy. Havoc played out on this peaceful Paris day.

The chaos of blood, screams and a falling chair subsided after the initial shock. The injuries were only minor and quickly cleaned up.

I cling to this memory, as much as I had clung to my dolly, and plunge through the alleys of time, extracting the many pieces of my existence.

I also must tell you that writing a memoir is like riding a ghost train. You pay at birth, get on the rickety open train and ride through dark tunnels with ghosts of the past popping out to scare the daylights out of you. Now and again, wispy skeletal fingers of memory brush your face, and you keep going along in the darkness, until a break happens, and you roll out into the daylight to see people standing there mindlessly staring at you while waiting for their own ride. Then back you go into the tunnel of half-forgotten memories until a bony skeleton pulls another scream out of you.

I ache when I remember parts of my childhood when I often felt as if I were two different little girls: one that was defiant, poking out her tongue, thumbs on the side of her forehead and wiggling her fingers in a gesture of 'I don't care, you can all go away', or the defeated little girl standing head bowed in the corner, hands behind her back, alienated from the rest of the class of carefree kids busy with everyday nothingness.

It wasn't my choice to emerge at a time when the war was exploding across Europe, and the myriads of people, including my parents, were running for their lives. According to my mother, I didn't want to arrive in the world.

Oh for goodness' sake! Don't let me get morbid at this early stage of our relationship! I write, you read. I tell you my story and sadly, you don't get to tell me yours.

If I knew for sure that there was a God, I would say, 'Hey, mister or madam, couldn't you have tried a little harder, couldn't you have made life less complicated? Couldn't you have left pain, disease and killing out of it all? Did you really have to try it out to see how humans react to your experiments? And did we really need to hear some pompous preaching about being given free will?'

It's taken me a long time to figure out how everything happened; why the people who came into my life appeared, went, stayed, taught me, gave me, took from me and left me with more questions than answers. I'm writing this book to make sense of it all, to share with you its most challenging parts, and mostly, to tell you about the one person who took up a quarter of my existence and barrelled me through the greatest lessons I had to learn. This was the man who brought me music, pain, tears and excitement.

By the time I met him, I was old enough to know better than to go chasing pretty butterflies over unknown walls into another kind of existence.

My mother's fears and the challenges of her illiteracy constrained me. Flitting about was my way of escaping the boredom of an ordinary life.

My memory is pregnant with his music, born every moment that his fingers touched the keyboard.

*

I can't imagine living in a world without music, notes filling the air, drifting into my ears like fingers grabbing the emotional layers of my being.

Some people just listen to music, others create it. I did both, and inside that world, I found many creative individuals.

My brother Phillip was responsible for the first song I remember when he came home with a relic gramophone that had a very large funnel. Out of it tumbled the deep voice of Paul Robeson, singing 'Old Man River', in a language I didn't understand. Phillip told me it was English and that the man whose voice magically floated in the air was black, same as his friend who often came for dinner and played hide-and-seek with me – not many places to hide in the one dining room that served as an all-purpose living space.

Evocative folk songs reflect the places of our origins, making us prone to emotional outbursts when hearing an old melody. I return to my roots when I hear '*Oif Dem Pripitchik*', an old Yiddish song that my father taught me. It's about a rabbi teaching little children the ABC in front of a warm fireplace.

No one in my family was musical, not even one straggly singer. However, there was a friend of my father's who came to us every Sunday morning to play cards with him. They had a glass of vodka, played *bollot* and had lunch. Somehow, I remember that he was called Mister Aronovich, except that he created a family fuss when he offered to sing at my cousin's wedding and afterwards asked for payment. The following Sunday, when he came to our apartment to play cards, my father stood in the doorway and stonily called him a *schnorrer* (a kind of sponger); they never played cards again. Everyone agreed, however, that the man had a good voice.

My father promised to send me to violin lessons, but it was just a promise and never came to fruition. Luckily, it didn't happen, because I can imagine the agonies that my family would have had to go through listening to hours of practice. Maybe a few interested refugee mice might have stuck around.

My mother loved opera; it had been part of her upbringing in Germany, and one of the melodies she sometimes sang during housework was from the operetta *Die Fledermaus*. Her off-tune warbling could drive anyone bats. Woo! A *fledermaus* is a bat. She sounded much better when she sang old Yiddish songs.

The notes tumbled through my life, preparing me for an eclectic taste in music; my collections included many genres, singers, bands, loud, soft, melodic, invasive, rock, country, vocals, classical; whatever took my fancy at the time. Popular songs from the charts, lyrics that had meaning, tunes which haunted and noises that defied description. I entered the new age with environmental sounds of birds, waterfalls, crickets and who knows what else that roamed the forests and fields. I had to learn to move beyond my childhood nightmares and go through a lot of growing up.

*

2 – War and Peace

> Observe constantly that all things take place by change and accustom thyself to consider that the nature of the Universe loves nothing so much as to change the things which are, to make new things like them.
> Marcus Aurelius

Sirens screamed behind me and the more I tried to get away from them, the more they chased me up the street, around a turn into the next street. I dodged cars and still, the howling noise followed me, around another sharp corner. The relentless pursuit continued until I was cornered in an open car park, and when I looked in my rear vision mirror, I saw an unmarked sedan with several men inside. One of them ambled out and came to the driver's side. He tried to open my door, but I had locked it.

Irritated, I shouted out to him, 'Who are you? What do you want?'
'Police. Open your door.'
'Show me your badge.'
Standoff. I was trapped, I had a moment of panic when the officer fished inside his clothes, pulled out his badge, and held it up.

I felt safe enough to roll the window down to ask, 'What do you want, officer? I wasn't doing anything – that is, until you started chasing me.'

'Open your boot.'

'What for?'

'You seem to be in a mighty hurry, young lady. You beeped the car in front of you and forced the driver to go through a red light.'

'Was there a red light? I thought he was just difficult. Is that all, officer? And, why do you want to look in my boot?'

'We've just had a complaint that a thief rushed out of the shopping centre and seeing you're in such a hurry…'

I laughed, 'Is that all?' I popped open the boot. 'You can have a look. I don't steal things.'

First, he looked in the boot, then at my licence and smiled. 'Do you make a habit of being chased by police sirens?'

I felt more relaxed. 'No, officer, not recently,' and the whole incident was over.

But it wasn't, not for me, not inside the compartments of my old memories of sirens, fear and escape.

This time I was a grown-up woman living in Australia, a long time and distance away from the origins of my fears. Perhaps these were the remnants left in me that had created my defiance toward authority.

*

Before the bombs poured from the sky, the sounds of sirens bombarded Paris, warning the inhabitants to run for shelter, mostly to the closest underground Metro.

Who would want to be born at a time like this, when hell's demons went trampling all over my birthplace, leaving death in their footprints? I really didn't want to arrive there and battled my mother's womb for a long time before I finally emerged.

This was not a time for music; the air filled with the sounds of Paris being ripped apart gave reason for my reluctance to enter this world.

The war over, my parents and our family often talked about those harsh years, of fear, running, hiding, leaving the city for safer places.

They wanted to remind me, and themselves, that we were the fortunate ones who had survived all the horrors, and were lucky to still be alive.

We escaped Paris with a few pieces of clothing thrown hastily into a battered suitcase. My parents talked about the dangerous train journey through the centre of France, and how every now and again, the Gestapo boarded the train to check personal papers, and anyone who looked suspicious was hauled off and taken somewhere for interrogation.

Fear was the common companion on that train as it tore across the countryside, taking its fodder of people with their meagre possessions into places away from the bombed battle zones of the capital city.

Small groups of our family members dispersed throughout the train in case one of us would be taken from our journey, never to be seen again. This was because my family decided that no matter what, some of us had to stay alive to create future generations.

Cramped together with other passengers in our carriage, our little group, my father, mother, an elderly grandmother and a few-weeks-old me, were travelling with fake papers that stated we were from Brittany, France.

A rat-infested barn in the soft French countryside was our new home until the end of the war. Too often, the rats ran with careless impunity across the overhead beams, long tails hanging over the edges, terrifying me with their twitching, whiskered noses and round little eyes looking down at me. My father told me they were kittens and were very frightened of us because we were so big and made a lot of noise, and because Papa said so, I lost my fear.

Funny how what we learn as kids stays with us. These days, when the odd rat runs across the beams of my veranda, I am perfectly at ease with it.

My father, who was clever with his hands, had a few makeshift tools, and with these, he made all kinds of things for the locals: soup ladles, fry pans, rolling pins, plant holders, bowls and an occasional coal bin. He exchanged them for fresh produce: milk, eggs, cheese, vegetables and fruit. They provided my mother with enough ingredients for her to create decent meals.

Throughout my growing-up years, I heard these fractured stories.

We didn't return to Paris until the end of the war when everyone picked up all the broken pieces of themselves to reconstruct their tomorrows.

My parents found a small two-bedroom first-floor flat at the end of a cobblestone courtyard in the suburb of Mairie des Lilas. It had a living room and a separate kitchen with a fuel stove, and no bathroom; the toilets were down the stairs and in the courtyard. I vaguely remember my mother carrying our family's potty downstairs to empty in the communal toilets. On the way, we passed our neighbours from upstairs; they were heading in the same direction. Their young son, Pierrot, was with them; he was my first crush. Walking alongside parents carrying full potties was excruciatingly embarrassing for six-year-olds.

We washed in a bowl of heated water and had weekly showers at the local bathhouse.

There was no privacy living in a cramped space with my mother, father, brother and my five-year-old cousin Louisa, who sometimes stayed with us and peed in the bed.

A short walk away was the next suburb of Porte des Lilas; my father established his small sheet metal atelier, where he made coal bins, baths and other tin items. He was a craftsman, not a businessman, and could never afford to buy me toys, so he took the time to craft for me, out of metal, a doll's table and chairs, and an entire crockery set, which I loved. Other times, he proudly gave me second-hand gifts he bought at the local flea market, old half-used paint tins, raggedy dolls, even an egg timer, which I thought was great until my mother took it away to use for its original purpose.

For my mother, he made rolling pins, baking trays and creative pieces out of copper and pewter: vases, flowerpots and a variety of household ornaments. Dad made all these items inside his workshop with its rich smells of old iron, rivets, hammers and other tools. After cutting pieces of metal, and pounding them into shape, my father put on his protective glasses and gloves, then lit a blue flame that came spurting out of the acetylene torch as it melted the bonding metal into useful and beautiful objects.

The smell of rusty metal still brings back the memories of my childhood and my father's magical workshop. I spent a lot of time there, watching him, or tinkering with odd pieces of metal, or scribbling in a huge ledger in his minuscule office.

The memories of the war lingered. Everyone was still recovering from its horror years, having lost their families, friends, homes and the whole life they had before. The scars lingered for too many years and played inside the emotional playgrounds of grown-ups and children.

At night, my nightmares filled with German soldiers and packs of wolves rushing out from behind the bedroom door, until the screams and tears of my fears woke me up. My father hugged me back to sleep.

So many people had lived through all of its death and horrors, followed by food scarcity and the rebuilding of lives that would never be the same again.

Anne Skyvington

Anne Skyvington received a Postgraduate Master Degree in Creative Writing from the University of Technology, Sydney, in 2000. She had already completed an MA in French Language and Literature at the University of Sydney in 1980. Both degrees have informed much of her writing style and craft by emphasising the importance of linguistic issues of textuality.

Currently she is the convenor of a writing group, Waverley Writers (part of Friends of Waverley Library), in which peer feedback is given in a supportive atmosphere. Before that, she was the convenor of Bondi Writers Group for several years.

Anne has been keeping a creative writing blog, focusing on the craft of writing for ten years, and has recently upgraded it to a self-hosted site. She has published many of her short stories, poems and book reviews on her personal blog, and has been published on other websites and in literary magazines. Awards for short story competitions through the Fellowship of Australian Writers have been attained from 2008 onwards.

She is interested in a wide range of topics and subject matters, from creativity through to psychological health, mysticism, travel and philosophy; she sees herself as a supporter of the underdog. Her completed manuscripts include a novel, *Karrana*, and a memoir, *River Girl*.

My writing journey

I started off writing for therapeutic reasons, keeping a diary of my travels overseas, and re-creating memories of childhood, with the intention of healing from psychological wounds. Eventually, I studied the features of creative writing at university, where I participated in feedback groups in order to improve my style and structure. When I retired from full-time teaching, I started a blog and practised writing creatively, including short stories and memoir. When I decided it was time to try my hand at writing a novel, I decided to find a small feedback group.

I was with Randwick Writers' Group at its inception, along with four other people, and I stayed with the group during the first two years. Being a member enabled me to exchange chapters for feedback, and to conceive of, and to finish, the first draft of a novel within about one year. After meeting with the group on a fortnightly basis, and offering chapters of *Karrana* for feedback, I had completed my first novel, compiled of forty chapters, amounting to eighty thousand words.

On showing my first draft to a couple of people, I realised that it required drastic structural improvements. At this stage, I felt what I needed was a 'macro approach' to edits, rather than the ongoing 'sentence level' corrections that the group word limit – segments of no more than two to three thousand words – required. To further improve my novel, I engaged a structural editor, which was a mistake at this early stage. What I should have sought was a manuscript assessment from a reputable editor, one who understood linguistic textuality issues. It has taken me until this time, four years later, to find such a person through Writing NSW.

A final word

I am forever grateful to the members of Randwick Writers' Group for enabling me to finish the first draft of my first-ever novel. Writing a novel is difficult, and a great deal of learning takes place during the activity. I have learnt a lot! Now, back to the drawing board.

☙

The following excerpts from *Karrana*, set in 1940s country NSW, are chosen to demonstrate that questions related to the macro-level of the novel were more important and relevant than sentence-level edits or chapter-length edits, once the first draft was completed, or preferably during the writing of the first draft.

The first excerpt is an early draft. Members suggested, helpfully, that I should set the novel at the end of the Second World War, instead of during it. At this stage, I did not know where I was going with the story, and what the main theme was. What should the beginning 'promise' in terms of the ending of the novel? What was the novel about? The main theme or themes? Single POV or Multiple POV? The latter would risk a slide into omniscient narrative point of view, now unpopular in publishers' eyes.

In the second excerpt, I decided, at this (later) stage, to fill out the character of Bridie O'Toole: to make her into a more rounded persona, crediting her with positive characteristics that balanced the negatives, and making her fit in a little more with country life on the land. At the same time, I wanted to add themes that pointed towards the ending of the novel: thereby fulfilling the promise set up in the beginning. These included the war refugee theme, Bridie wanting more, needing to go on learning, wanting a better house, seeking physical satisfaction, finding a perfect love. (Irony!) In other words, the main theme of the novel might be Bridie's journey to find fulfilment in her life. If I'd known this earlier on, the writing journey would have been a great deal easier for me.

In the third excerpt, I decided that perhaps the novel should begin at a different point in the first chapter – for example, getting ready for the dance. This would be apt, since one of the early thrusts of the novel was Bridie's push to find an appropriate mate.

In the fourth excerpt, from the second chapter, both main characters' points of view are intermingled. This needed to be reviewed and resolved. I researched multiple points of view and how to achieve it without head-hopping – that is, switching between points of view in the same passage. You can find an example or two of this error in the excerpt.

In the fifth excerpt, after deciding to show everything through the eyes of Bridie O'Toole, I rewrote the chapters with this in mind. This involved more dialogue when Will was in scene. However, this proved to be problematical in terms of the authenticity of the dialogue at this early stage.

In the sixth excerpt, I realised that some of my best writing was linked to the male protagonist, Will Featherstone. So, back to the drawing board: how to use multiple viewpoints without sliding into an omniscient point of view? The final answer was to favour Bridie as the main protagonist, while giving Will precedence in some chapters, and allowing him to share the POV with Bridie, within well-delineated segments at certain other points also. This excerpt is an example of how I managed to focus the POV on Will in an early chapter of my novel. The second draft was well under way at this stage.

*

1: The Beginning

Bridie perched on the veranda railing of the farmhouse and watched the orange orb settling in the west beyond the house. A pink afterglow lit up the horizon with a last exotic flair, revealing the silhouettes of banana trees and bangalow palms. The air smelt earthy and humid. High up on the peaks large black birds circled. Swifts. A sign of bad weather to come. Storms sometimes shook the old farmhouse, sending Bridie screaming along the unsealed track to the Hooleys' more solid dwelling on the banks of the Karrana River.

'Come in, dearie,' Mrs Hooley would say in her kindly voice. 'No need to be afraid. It'll soon pass.'

Like a needle stuck in the groove of a record, Bridie's mind returned to the poverty surrounding her. It went there often. True, the house was a step up from the dirt-floored shack that had once stood in the paddock further down. But this run-down dairy farm signalled the rut her family was stuck in. If only Dadda, before he died, had encouraged them to make the most of their schooling days. One of the brothers could have used his head to do something with the hundred acres. Instead, they were still just making ends meet. Spending every penny they earned from the small herd of milkers.

Her thoughts turned now to the outside lavatory that she had to endure each time she needed to 'go'. Huge green tree frogs, throbbing in high-up crevices, blinked down at her with yellow eyes. And ugly black widow spiders called redbacks hid in the wood heap out the back. Worse still were the black snakes that slithered in long grass on crimson bellies, ready to spring up and give you a deadly bite if you trod on them.

Oh, how she yearned for a civilised place in which to live. She wasn't one of these country girls who loved dogs and horses. Stella, who she'd gone to school with, was like that. Stella had been one of the smart girls, who stayed on at school and went to secretarial college.

If only Mumma and Sid had agreed, Bridie knew she could have gone on too. The nuns at the convent had encouraged her.

'What's the use of schooling for a girl?' Sid had said. And Mumma had been pleased to have the extra help at home.

Farm animals, she thought, her nose twitching. Smelly, germ-carrying pigs and cows, they're all right in their place, which is outside. She was forever washing her hands and her clothes, and bathing every day in the enamel tub to get rid of the grime and dust brought in on her brothers' boots and work clothes.

'You're a good-looker, Bridie,' Cyclone Johnny said when he came across her standing on the veranda. He'd been saying this to her since she was an infant, the first girl born after six sons. She hardly understood the words at first, until one day her mother caught her looking into a mirror, saying, 'Yes, I have a pretty face.' This became part of family folklore and led to teasing.

In spite of herself, the syllables that slid from her brother's tongue sent waves of pleasure throughout her body. She savoured the taste of flattery. Her looks were her saving grace that would lift her out of this godforsaken place, steeped in ignorance and boredom. She knew that she could make something of herself if given the chance.

Johnny had an announcement to make. 'I won the race again, this time pitched against Will Featherstone. He's pretty fast too. From the east side. His old man's loaded.'

'That's good, Johnny. All the girls will be throwing themselves at you again at the dance. You and Sid going to it tomorrow night?'

'Sure thing, Bridie. Wouldn't miss it for the world.'

With his star status as a champion cyclist, Johnny fancied himself as a bit of a ladies' man with his playboy looks. He was wiry and self-consciously handsome, his brown hair sculpted into waves with the aid of Brylcreem.

He showed Bridie the earring from one of his girlfriends that he'd kept as a trophy on the mantelpiece in the brothers' room since his last outing.

'Johnny, that's awful,' shrieked Bridie. 'I'd hate a man to do that to me.' Her eyes flashed as she faced him now. 'You're disgusting when it comes to women, Johnny. Dadda used to call you a "black sheep" and "loafer", said you didn't know the meaning of a hard day's work. I stuck up for you then, but now I think I agree with him.' Her voice, which had been rising in anger, dropped, as Johnny hung his head. 'Trouble is, you're nothing when you're not behind the bars of a racing bike.'

Johnny grinned at her. 'We'll take you along to the dance, Bridie. Introduce you to some of the lads.'

'Yes, Mumma will only let me go if I'm with you and Sid. She's so old-fashioned. I'm nineteen already, for goodness sake.'

'We'll look after you, Bridie. What's the word? Chaperons, isn't it?'

*

2: Reworked Beginning

Bridie O'Toole perched on the back veranda steps and watched the sun dipping voluptuously into the mountains. Please don't let it rain tonight, she prayed silently. Not tonight of all nights. She glanced back at the grey clouds looming up from the east, spreading their menace over the tin roof. Returning her gaze towards the far horizon, she whispered 'infinity', as the hills gobbled up the last rays of the sun. A sharp tat-a-tat interrupted her reveries.

Her mother, standing at the kitchen stove, had flicked her tea towel and clicked on the window pane. 'Get back in, why don'chu, girl?' she shrilled. 'It's the last race of the day just finishing, an' you can come in an' have some tea.'

Two of her brothers, Johnny and Billy, were a bit deaf. Every Saturday afternoon, they glued themselves to the wireless to listen to the races. The caller chanting like a maniac. Static from the black bakelite wireless assailing her senses through the thin walls of the house. She would try to block her ears with her fists. The noise, worse than the dirt, the smells and the insects.

She knew to obey her mother, though. Especially tonight. The last thing she wanted was to spoil her chances of going to the dance. Now that she'd turned eighteen, she could go. With conditions. She could go, so long as her brothers kept an eye on her. Mumma had spoken.

Snippets from the evening news caught her attention. Camp survivors coming by ship to Australia. Who were these Jewish refugees? If only she'd been allowed to stay at school longer. Maybe then she'd understand many things better.

War and fear were behind them now. Taking a bit longer to peter out down here in the Pacific. The future looked brighter. She'd gleaned that much from all the men's talk at Hilltop over the last four years.

An orangey-pink afterglow lit up the horizon with a last exotic flair. High up on the peaks large dark birds circled. Swifts, a sign of bad weather to come.

One part of her loved the farm and nature with a passion. She'd always carry the country with her. It was in her veins. Her other side was a headstrong filly that wanted to get away. Always two sides. Was everyone like that she wondered: two sides?

Like a needle stuck in the groove of a record, Bridie's mind went now to the dreariness of the dairy farm. It went there often. Especially since Dadda's passing. The run-down farmhouse signalled the rut her family was stuck in. If only one of the six brothers could have used his head to do something more with the hundred acres. Mumma, with the eldest, Ned, was only just making ends meet. Spending every penny they earned from the small herd of milkers.

She thought of poor Johnny, amid the blood and guts at the local abattoirs each week day. And Billy with his stammer, working his guts out for all of them. Two brothers had left home to go off to war. One of them, Charlie, had not returned. Went off to fight in the trenches up north. She pictured his dear face. Lying in the mud.

Irresistibly, the image of young men vying for her attention, intervened. Hopefully there'd be a few leftover soldier types at the dance. All the boys she'd known before were from the pony camps. Roughly spoken, freckle-faced youths from country properties.

From the safe hub of the veranda, she wondered if real bad weather was brewing out west. Storms sometimes shook the old farmhouse, sending Bridie screaming along the unsealed track to the neighbours' more solid dwelling on the banks of the Karrana River.

She picked up more news snippets coming from the dining room now. About Prime Minister John Curtin, maybe the anniversary of his death. Died from a broken heart, Mumma had said, often. He'd led the country through the last years of the war, then gave up the ghost, just as it was ending. Tragic, really.

Here on the dairy farm, they'd felt safe from the war. Mumma often said how the Japs were real cruel to our boys. But Bridie'd known that the war would never come to Hilltop. She just knew certain things in her heart, a bit like how the cows knew when it was time to come back for milking. It had touched them, sure, like her favourite brother lost-in-action.

But the Garden of Eden had remained unaltered.

She remembered that she'd have to endure the outside lavatory now. Before it turned dark. Huge green tree frogs, throbbing in high-up crevices there, blinked down at her with yellow eyes. She shuddered as she tiptoed along the grassy path, cringing at the thought of the black widow spiders called red backs that hid in the wood heap out the back. Worse still were the snakes that slithered in long grass on crimson bellies, ready to spring up and bite if you trod on them.

A few mod cons like in the *Women's Weekly* magazines and a stylish house wouldn't hurt. That's for sure. She was forever washing her hands and face in the basin. Trying to get rid of the dirt.

*

3: Where to Begin?

Bridie slid into her pink satin dress with the burgundy sash. She pushed her toes into high-heeled shoes, which added three inches to the five-foot-three nature had given her. Posing as she had seen the stars on the big screen do, Bridie looked at her figure from all angles. Perfect. She sat at the dressing table and painted her lips bright red. Pursing her mouth for full effect, she fluttered her long-curled eyelashes at her image in the mirror. The eyebrows needed re-shaping one more time, and she fiddled with the bobby-pins that fastened the roll at the crown. Lovely. Half closing her eyes to capture what someone else would see, she stood up and tossed her dark brown hair, watching it cascade around her shoulders. She pulled her waist in and poked out her sharp-pointed breasts. Just like Vivien Leigh or one of the other Hollywood stars.

Johnny will say that I look like a million dollars, she thought. This was the opposite message that her mother, Eliza O'Toole, plump and pot-bellied in middle age, had tried to plant in her mind. 'He wouldn't want you, too good for us,' she'd said of one of the town's well-to-do bachelors.

Bridie knew better. What she wanted, she couldn't properly put into words. She'd heard the word uncouth. A couth man…whatever that meant…someone with manners and good looks. She intended to use her own advantages to the fullest. But would they attract the right one?

'Ugh,' Bridie scoffed, as she heard Ned spitting over the veranda railing at that moment.

He'd decided to go to the dance. They'd have to come back early for the milking at first light. Jerseys mooing in the dark to be relieved of full udders.

She went out to the dining room to pirouette in front of her mother, who she could see through the open door. Still sweating in front of the wood stove in the kitchen.

'Mumma, how do I look?' Bridie did a twirl for her.

'Not bad, though I say so myself,' Mumma said, looking up and wiping her forehead, 'seeing as I ran it up on the old Singer.'

'Yeah, thanks Mumma,' Bridie said, 'don't stay up for us, will you?'

'Just you make sure an' come straight home with Ned and Johnny. Don't want any goings-on in back lanes afterwards.'

'Yeah, Mumma, I know, but I'm not a child any more.'

'You'll do as I say while you're under my roof,' her mother, red-faced from the heat in the kitchen, sighed, 'and have a bite to eat before you go out.'

'I'm not hungry, Mumma,' Bridie called out as she turned away, 'I'll have some bread and butter when I get back.'

Noises were already coming from the men's room, a dark interior space where the brothers kept their clothes in wardrobes, their personal belongings in a chest of drawers. They slept on camp beds in sleep-outs on the verandas that circled the rickety timber house.

*

4: The Risk of Head-hopping

Bridie, in the pink calf-length dress, tight-belted at the waist, raised up on stiletto heels, was the belle of the ball, her dark hair twirling. Will

Featherstone had spotted her as soon as she came into the hall. He was muscular with moulded features and a sensitive nature that he tried to hide beneath his felt hat. His thick dark hair had a russet tinge in the sunlight. A giant of a man, towering over most of the other men at the dance, his eyes lit up now with the spark that others noticed when he was happy: the giveaway sign of his innermost feelings.

Bridie had no time to accept or to refuse. He swept her up in strong arms and guided her round the dance floor with confident strides.

She looked up into his shiny face and realised that he was handsome. A thrill ran though her body at the sight of the craggy face beaming down at her, hazel eyes, and…those lips… She couldn't take her eyes off his mouth. Something about the intelligent bearing of the man. His sense of self-importance; something manly and gentle all at the same time. So different from her loud-mouthed brothers. She felt that she had seen him somewhere before and had noticed him. He wheeled her around the farthest edge of the outside of the floor towards the door. Once outside, on the steep bank of the Karrana River, he grabbed her in a craggy embrace and crushed his dry lips against her wet ones.

'I don't even know your name,' Bridie stammered, savouring the touch of his lips, dry and salty on hers and secretly wanting more.

'Will Featherstone. It doesn't matter. I know you, Bridie O'Toole.'

At that moment, Sid and Johnny came out and joined them.

'Bridie, this is Will Featherstone, my racing mate I told you about.'

'Cyclone Johnny,' said Will, shaking his hand with vigour. As if he and Bridie had not, a few minutes earlier, been locked together like one, by an irresistible force.

Bridie blushed as she turned her wide pools of eyes, fringed with black lashes towards Will. 'Is that how you knew who I was?'

'I've seen you for a long time, Bridie. I've always known you,' he added.

'You're from the north side, then, Will? Haven't seen you about our side at all.'

'Yes, I live in Karrana on the river bank.'

'Lucky you, then, Will Featherstone! That's where I'd like to live!'

She was nearly going to say 'bugger' when she thought better of it. He was a well-bred sort of young man.

He was thinking about how he loved the farm-maid look of her underneath the make-up, with her fresh lips and lovely eyes wide as pools. 'Another dance?' And he swept her up in those manly arms once again and felt her perfume infuse his body like heady flowers on his mother's vines.

'I saw you once, years ago.' he said, a lucid image infused with light startling him, with its sudden apparition as from a dream. 'You were walking along River Street outside St Josephs' wearing a navy uniform and a little beret perched on your head.'

'That sounds like me,' she said. 'But how could you remember after seeing me just that once?'

'I couldn't take my eyes off you, even then. At eleven or so you must have been.'

Bridie felt a ripple of pleasure flow through her body. It all fitted in so well with the image she had always had of herself. Everyone in the family telling her how lovely she was. And the jealousy from other girls in her class. She even revelled in their envy, seeing it as further proof of her superiority, rather than as a nasty yoke around her neck.

He was already thinking about how he could ask her out. But he wasn't really thinking at all. His thoughts taken over by the scent of her. The idea of 'head-over-heels' became clear to him then at that moment. These feelings were different from anything that he had ever experienced before. Nothing, not his steady home life with his three plain sisters and his steady-going parents had in any way opened him up to this possibility. She felt good in his arms; she felt right. It was the sense of touch, like the feelings he got when he was out in the bush with the quiet all around him and the smell of wattle and eucalypt and the soft feel of the horse against his thighs.

And he knew at that moment that he was trapped, as surely as a prisoner in a cell at the gaol, caught like a butterfly on a pin, a fly in a spider's web, or a bee in the heady scent of a rose. It was a prison where he would go voluntarily, and no one, not even his parents, would force him away from this lovely fate.

*

5: A Single POV

Bridie, in the pink calf-length dress, tight-belted at the waist, and raised up on stiletto heels, was the belle of the ball, her dark hair twirling. She'd noticed the man, towering over most of the other men at the dance, as she'd entered the hall. It was hard not to notice him.

She had no time to accept or to refuse his invitation; he'd spotted her as soon as she came into the hall, and swept her up in strong arms. Guided her around the dance floor with confident strides. She could feel his heart pounding against her breast, as he swirled her around the corners of the dance floor, holding her tight.

She looked up into his shiny face and realised that he was good-looking. Muscular with moulded features. His thick dark hair had a russet tinge. His eyes lit up now with a spark.

A thrill ran though her body at the sight of the rugged features beaming down at her. Warm hazel eyes and…those lips… She couldn't take her eyes off his mouth. There was something about the intelligent bearing of the man, his self-importance; something manly and gentle all at the same time. So different from her loud-mouthed brothers. She felt that she had seen him somewhere before, had noticed him. He wheeled her around the farthest edges of the floor towards the door. Once outside, on the steep bank overlooking the river, he grabbed her in a fierce embrace and crushed his dry lips against her wet ones.

'I don't even know your name,' Bridie stammered, savouring the touch of his mouth, dry and salty, and secretly wanting more. She pulled back.

'Will Featherstone. It doesn't matter. I know you, Bridie O'Toole.'

'H…how?' she whispered. 'Where?'

At that moment, Johnny came out and joined them.

'This is my...brother,' Bridie shook a little as she tried to say names. 'Will Feather...'

'I know, Bridie. He's my cycling mate,' Johnny laughed.

'Cyclone Johnny,' said Will, shaking his hand with vigour. As if he and Bridie had not, a few minutes earlier, been locked together like one. An overpowering force.

Bridie blushed as she turned her wide pools of eyes, fringed with black lashes, towards Will. 'Is that how you knew who I was?'

'I've seen you for a long time, Bridie. I think...like...always...I've seen you around the town. You went to the convent, didn't you?'

'Yes, that is where I went,' Bridie exclaimed. 'How did you know? Where did you go to school, Will?'

'Karrana Public School. Then to the high school.'

'You're from the north side, then? Haven't seen you about these parts at all.'

'Yes, I live in Karrana,' he said, indicating with his hand, 'directly opposite here...as the crow flies.' He was pointing towards the river, way off through the gum trees, the same river she loved so well back at Hilltop.

'Lucky you, then, Will Featherstone. That's where I'd...like to live.' She was nearly going to say 'bugger', when she thought better of it. He seemed a well-bred sort of young man.

'I saw you once, years ago,' he said, a faint image, infused with light, seeming to startle him. 'You were walking along River Street, outside St Joseph's wearing a navy tunic and a little beret perched on your head.'

'That sounds like me,' she said, 'but...how could you remember, after seeing me just that once?'

'I couldn't take my eyes off you, even then. Twelve or so you must have been.'

Bridie smiled. It all fitted in so well with the image she had of herself. Everyone in the family telling her how lovely she was. With her long dark hair. A swan neck, they said. And the jealousy from other girls in her class. She even revelled in their envy, seeing it as further proof of her assets, rather than as something mean and nasty.

'Another dance?' And he swept her up in his solid arms once again, and she felt her perfume infuse his body, like heady flowers on her mother's vines.

After that, no man managed to come between Bridie and Will.

As they danced, and in between dances, Bridie told him about living with her mother and brothers since her father died five years ago. How her mother had ordered her older brother to take over the role of father, and how he watched her like a hawk. 'Dadda was a lot easier,' she said. 'Let me do whatever I wanted.'

Will told her about his family: his mother, father and two sisters. He told her how he worked in his father's garage, behind the counter, and that he hated it. 'Dad tries at every turn to show me neither fear nor favour,' he said. He'd taught Will how to swim as a three-year-old by diving into the river with the child on his back. 'I thought he wanted to drown me,' he said, 'but it toughened me up, I can tell you. When I was fifteen, I could dive from the footbridge into the river, a great yawning drop below.'

Bridie imagined the mother, anxious, running to take the petrified infant from her husband's back.

'Dad favours the girls,' he said, 'always has. Mum's more for me, but I just want to get away, become independent.'

'Why's that?' Bridie asked, wondering at the force behind the words.

'Mum's always wanting to know who I'm with, what I'm doing.'

'Oh.'

*

6: A Secondary POV

When he got to Halfway Creek, he had to stop to catch his breath. It was pitch-black now, with the stars blotted out by the height of the trees and the lay of the land. Some bush creatures, probably a wallaby or a rabbit, scuttled away on the other side of the bridge. An owl made an eerie sound like a warning coming from on high.

Will shivered. He wheeled his bike across the bridge and leant it against a tree on the opposite side. He would take a quick gulp of water before embarking on the second leg of his journey. He was a lot tireder than he thought he would be.

As he got closer to the creek bed, he noticed something strange. A light that was moving in a bizarre way parallel to the road, coming from the direction in which he had cycled: like a small meteor, only it was moving above the grassy culvert. He tried to reason with himself about the light source and what it might be. He took a few steps back towards his bike. The light swerved off into the bush, dodging or going right through tree trunks; he wasn't quite sure which.

'Who's there?' No response. He took a few steps towards the creek. 'Who in God's name is there?' He was shouting now. No one. Just the light moving in a bizarre way.

He felt a shiver of fear like a whiplash strike through his body. Geez, he didn't want to be a sissy overtaken by fear. Even a rabbit knew how to shake off the fear after being caught in a spotlight.

He started to shake. His teeth chattered. He felt he might shake himself to death. The light was moving back slowly this time towards the bridge. He took another step towards the creek. He was no longer thirsty. He just wanted to know what the hell it was. It seemed to gather speed as he got nearer, then flashed off in a different direction.

Suddenly, he knew what he wanted. He wanted to get the hell out of there! Get away from the creek and out of there as quickly as he could.

The bloody light seemed to be stalking him. Just as he got to his bike, the light appeared to dive down into the water beneath the bridge, and disappeared, as if it had emerged from there.

Will didn't stop to investigate further. He jumped on his racing bike and sped, hell-for-bloody-leather away at full speed. He never looked back. Every nerve in his body tingled and he felt that he had escaped with the skin of his clattering teeth. Another second and he was a goner! From what? He had no idea.

Now it was fear that gave him the momentum. He sped the remaining seven kilometres faster than he had ridden in his life before. He was panting and gasping for air like a stranded perch as he pulled up at Honeysuckle Cottage. He knew that his face was white as a bleeding ghost. He waited to get his breath back and regain colour before going inside.

It was something that he would carry with him forever, buried deep within, something that he would not share with a living soul. For fear of being thought mad. Or worse: a gutless, fear-craven sheila.

Geraldine Star

My writing journey

My writing focuses on characters and themes in the Australian countryside. I was an avid reader who dreamt of distant lands but lived close to nature on a farm. The bush triggered my imagination.

Imagination

Imagination is a remarkable beast, a flighty bird-like quality started by the simplest thing: a conversation heard while travelling in a bus, a person with a different way of dressing or walking, an incident that may have happened years ago that comes back to haunt you. Listening to music, visiting an art gallery, taking long walks along the sea or in the bush. Travelling into your own depths can spark imagination. This capricious quality is a writer's dream, which sends you far away or makes you and your readers laugh at the absurdity of life.

The Australian bush lights my imagination: the gnarled nature of the trees and bushes, the subtle variegated colours of leaves and the vibrancy of flowers. The vastness of its landscape, the wooded mountains to the iron-red soils of the inland plains, its population clinging to the coastline provides an enormous palette to draw from. What a shock for early European settlers to find a world not so green and manicured. Indigenous people had cultivated and used this country for thousands of years, integrating their way of life and spiritual practices in order to survive. They are the people we should honour for their imagination and integrity in using this great land.

I was born in Sydney and went with my family to live on an irrigated sheep and wheat property near the Hay Plain when I was six.

It was a rude awakening. The terrain was flat as far as the eye could see with stands of timber dotted throughout. Kangaroos, emus and snakes roamed freely, even to the back door. We lived in a small cottage with no electricity, no running water and no phone. People consider this idyllic but relying on a kerosene fridge and lamps and buying drinking water was often fraught. It was a great place to develop an imagination. There were many interpretations from the shadows cast by lamps. We used photos from *National Geographic* magazines, torches and beer cans to build our own picture theatres under our beds. Living on an isolated farm with no bus to a secondary school meant I had to leave the bush for boarding school. It educated me off the land. I still can't muster sheep.

Reading

Thrust into an alien place in the countryside, my default became reading. The worlds of Biggles, the Famous Five, *Phantom* and *Superman* comics, the local papers, anything I could get my hands on, including newspaper wrappings from the fish and chips I devoured. In hindsight, there were few books written by Australian authors available and I remember a comic-like story describing the wonderful tennis talents of Evonne Goolagong, but it was from an English magazine. This changed when I got older and found Patrick White. His books resonated with how I saw the Australian bush and the larger-than-life characters it shaped. He became my inspiration, a well-known Australian novelist, a Nobel Prize winner in literature, who could transcend the parochialism of our society and write of the universal by using the backdrop of his home country. I laughed and cried, my imagination on fire; at last I could see the seeds that produced great works in my backyard. Since then, I have read widely across the globe and been entertained and inspired by different authors whom I have held in awe, but none have brought me back to my land like Patrick White did at that time.

Writing

My writing journey is dappled with bits here and there. I kept journals when I travelled and remember going to a beginner writers' workshop at Sydney University presented by a well-established author. I limped from this horrid experience vowing never to write again.

Later, I worked with the well-known award-winning First Nation writer Anita Heiss. Through the many books she has written and edited, she has showcased her culture, the touchstones being friendship and family, with anger and angst, love, joy and compassion. Her work is a leveller. It illustrates the profound and greatness in the benign and the everyday. She has forged an inspiring path not only for me, but also for many other Indigenous and non-Indigenous people.

Like many women, I didn't trust my ability to write, so decided that I needed further study, and undertook a Diploma in Creative Writing at the University of Technology in Sydney. This helped me to focus on theory and practice and put me in touch with the dynamics of contemporary writing.

After this course, I wrote short stories, one of which won the Bondi Writers Seagull Award. I was hooked on writing and wanted to spend more time developing my skills and story lines.

In early 2014, I undertook a writing master class with the Booker Prize winner Thomas Keneally, and *When We Have Wings* author Claire Corbett, to get further tips on the craft of writing. As a part of this workshop, Thomas offered words of wisdom and thought I should have a go at writing a novel.

Now I am a writer with a series of short stories and an unpublished manuscript in my kitbag, and another long narrative at first draft stage. My current focus is on getting some of my work published.

The importance of writers' groups

I have received invitations to be a member of two writers' groups, the Randwick Writers' Group and the Celestial Writers' Group. Each has a different emphasis and has provided me with support and encouragement at specific stages of my writing.

Belonging to two writing groups has been rewarding and has contributed to my growth as a writer. I wouldn't recommend it to writers who are just starting out. There is an enormous commitment to reading and giving constructive feedback to the other participants, and on preparing your own work. You must be brave.

Randwick Writers' Group

I joined Randwick Writers in 2014, following an invitation from the convenor, Dina Davis, and have been an active member since. The discipline of meeting every second week for a year provided me with the opportunity to write and receive timely feedback rather than wait for an editor or publisher to critique my work. At the end of the first year, I realised that I had completed the first draft of a sixty-thousand-word YA novel with the help of the members. The Comma Queens worked overtime to knock my grammar and punctuation into shape and offered ideas on how to expand my skills. In particular, my ability to write dialogue improved. Not only did my writing take on a new direction, but I also learnt how to give and receive feedback through the collaborative nature of the group. As budding authors, we exchanged the names of publishers and agents, passed on titles of books to read and writing courses to do, and encouraged each other to keep going when our paths felt difficult.

I have remained with Randwick Writers for my second novel, *Riding the Storm*, and the rewards have been great. Once again, this collaborative group has supported me. Some members have moved on but the core membership remains. The group now meets about once a month, so the deadlines are not as trying.

Celestial Writers' Group

Randwick Writers gave me the skills and experience I needed in order to take on this extra group.

I met the members of the Celestial Writers' Group when my work was shifting. I was listening to podcasts about craft. I was also seeking greater depth with characterisation. This involved exploring the inner worlds of my characters and the impact their emotional wounds might have on their behaviour.

This group has stretched my writing, making it more colourful and fun. They have helped me to pare down my scenes, making them more realistic. My characters have grown, and my writing has developed extra depth.

༄

The following excerpt from my novel *Riding the Storm* builds a picture of Mia's mother, Lisa, and their interactions when she visits her daughter in Canberra. Mia is reflecting on what transpired. The accident is raised early in the novel but the full description of what happened is not revealed before this chapter.

*

Lisa's visit from the US

The unfolding image exploded through her head. Recurring flashes, jagged and black, jolted her from her sleep. Her mother's whining voice grated. Her unrecognisable face reshaped by too many facelifts, her long ponytail streaked with grey and her hippy clothing left over from another era. Lisa, Californian chic with a Texan drawl and a whiff of her native accent.

Staring at the cracked upholstery lining on the Kombi's roof, Mia recalled the weird phone call.

'Hello, is that my gal?' said a woman's voice. She talked over a startled Mia. 'It's your Mom. I'm coming back to see you. Give me your email. I'll send the details.'

Then the diatribe began. She attacked everything: Mia's father; family members who Mia didn't know; Mia's decision to live in Australia; why she had not contacted or visited her. Mia held the phone away from her ear and stared into the distance. At the final click, she collapsed on the nearby couch.

Within two minutes, Mia's phone rang again. She sat up, looked at the unknown number, lay back down again, switched on the TV, and let the sound fill the room.

Months passed until one bleak blustery Canberra day there was a knock at Mia's door. She dropped the book she was reading. There on the other side of the security screen, stood a rather strange-looking woman with dark brown eyes accentuated by kohl. She wore bangles and a jauntily placed beret and was dressed in a long black skirt with cowboy boots. A three-quarter maroon silver-threaded coat hung from her shoulders.

'My darling... How are you?' The intruder flung her large purple-checked scarf around her neck.

Mia stood looking perplexed at this unfamiliar image.

'It's your Mom. Don't you recognise me?'

This woman didn't fit what Mia dreamed her mother would be like. She hadn't seen her since she was ten, and she'd arrived at an interesting part in the book she was reading.

'I told you I'd come,' the woman begged. 'Your father gave me your address.'

Mia slowly opened the door.

'Ah, that's better. Now I want a big hug.'

Mia closed her eyes and gritted her teeth as the tall woman folded her arms around her. There was no warmth in the hug.

For the next ten minutes, Lisa babbled about where she lived in the States, and about her new husband, Andy. Mia half listened, made them both a coffee, and put on Baaba Maal to soothe the intrusion to her day.

'Mia, switch off that rubbish. It reminds me of that dreary father of yours and living in Kenya.'

The music continued to play.

Mia tried to think of how she could get rid of her guest. She gathered her leotard and dancing shoes. 'I've got to go to my dancing class now. You must go, Lisa.'

'But I want to spend time with you, my darling daughter.'

Mia hissed through her teeth. 'Sorry, my friend Brad is coming to collect me. We'll have coffee before you leave.'

'I've lost your number. What is it?'

Mia wrote on an old envelope and shoved it at Lisa. 'When do you return home?'

'In about two weeks. I want to visit my old haunts first. My childhood farm, I'd like to see it.' Lisa wrapped the purple-checked scarf around her neck; it made her look even more theatrical. 'You could come with me. It's not far from here.'

Mia tried to remember when she'd last called Lisa 'Mom'. Never a mother! Too self-absorbed, too selfish to worry about her and her father. He always said, when he'd had too much to drink, that she married him for his money. He loved Lisa, but she played along until the next man came. He'd say he still loved her then his tears would flow. As a child, Mia tried to console him by giving him a hug but got sick of that.

With a shudder, she remembered reluctantly agreeing to go with 'Mom' on a jaunt to the farm where Lisa had grown up.

Mia closed the door, leant against it. 'My mother? She asked nothing about my life.' She burst into tears.

*

In the rented car, Mia's anxiety rose. She had no idea what to expect. A short woollen coat, a scarf, jeans and riding boots protected her against the cold, miserable weather, but not her mother. Ominous.

'Maybe I should drive. I know my way around Canberra,' said Mia.

'No, I grew up here and I can drive on the left-hand side of the road.'

There was a shaky start through the streets of Canberra. Mia closed her eyes and gripped the door handle.

As the city gave way to picturesque little farms, Lisa displayed a renewed sense of urgency. She leant towards Mia like a conspirator. 'Don't know why I'm going back. A horrid place. A family friend with a big pink nose sexually abused me at twelve. You never get over it. Damaged goods, as they say.'

Mia put her hands over her ears.

'Don't worry, I'll spare you the details. Yes, best revealed to an expensive therapist: I lay on one's couch for years.' Lisa punched the steering wheel with her hand. 'Therapy's an American sport. Do you go to one?' Lisa didn't wait for an answer. 'I went from man to man at uni. We all did in the seventies – that is, until I met your father. A kind man, too good for me.'

Mia turned her head and stared out the window while her mother continued her monologue.

After they had travelled for about an hour, Lisa said, 'This trip seems to be taking forever. It never took this long when I was a child.' She peered at a road sign when they reached a fork in the road and slammed her foot on the accelerator rather than the brake.

Next minute, Mia screamed as she saw her mother take the corner too fast on the wrong side of the road and felt the car rush towards a nearby fence. That was all she remembered.

Selected Readings

Writers from the group have found a range of books and authors' blogs that are useful references to help develop imagination and creativity, and to build the techniques of writing. This is a selection of readings that may be of help on the writing journey.

Books

Becoming a Writer – Dorothea Brande was far ahead of her time when she wrote this book, first published in 1934 and reissued in 1981. Instead of writing a nuts and bolts guide, she focused on the qualitative aspects: artistry, self-actualisation, the role of the unconscious mind, and more.

Bird by Bird: Some Instructions on Writing and Life – Anne Lamott's 1995 autobiographical writing guide, republished in 2008, is full of honest, humorous reflections about the writing life. It contains frank, funny admissions that give you permission to be human, too.

Dear Writer Revisited – written by Carmel Bird and first published in 1988 as *Dear Writer*, it was reissued in 2013. It is a series of letters to writers who submit manuscripts, with insights into the essence of the writer's art.

How Fiction Works – James Woods's book, published in 2008, is both a study of the techniques of story telling and an alternative history of the novel. He dissects the machinery of fiction, looking at such areas as characters, metaphors, beginnings and endings.

Make a Scene: Crafting a Powerful Story One Scene at a Time – Jordan Rosenfeld's 2007 guide to constructing a great story scene by scene analyses examples representing a wide variety of styles and types of scenes. Well-constructed vignettes must illustrate and employ the use of fictional aspects such as vivid characters, scenes, events, climax, resolution, plot and arc and so on.

Making Stories – published in 1993 and reprinted in 2001 by Kate Grenville and Sue Woolfe, this book shows ten acclaimed Australian authors at work. It painstakingly constructs their books from rough notes, dimly glimpsed ideas and trial and error.

Novelist's Essential Guide to Crafting Scenes – novelist and writing instructor Raymond Obstfeld emphasises how skilfully crafted scenes are the heart of a successful story. This comprehensive guide from 2000 is suitable for novices and experienced writers alike.

On Writing: a Memoir of the Craft – though much of Stephen King's 2000 tome, reprinted in 2012, is autobiographical, it also contains many useful tips for writers. These include technical matters such as grammar as well as thoughts about character and plot. A valuable element is a section that includes a rough draft and an edited draft of one of his stories. Even if you consider King a middlebrow writer, you can't deny that he is a master of his craft, and we should be so fortunate.

Self-editing for Fiction Writers: How to Edit Yourself Into Print – Renni Browne and Dave King's 1993 work focuses not on the craft of writing but on the next step: editing your own work. The authors discuss dialogue, interior monologue, exposition, point of view and other elements of story, with examples, exercises and checklists. It was republished in 2004.

Steering the Craft: Exercises and Discussions on Story Writing – based on a writing workshop offered by legendary science fiction author Ursula K. LeGuin, this 1998 collection of discussions and writing exercises includes such tasks as eschewing punctuation, adjectives and adverbs, and halving a story's word count.

The Artist's Way – Julia Cameron's 1991 book, reprinted in 2016, looks at developing creativity and how to master limiting beliefs, self-sabotage, fear and guilt to keep the creative process flowing. There is a twelve-week workbook. While this guide could be considered a self-help book it is also useful for freeing up the imagination and creativity.

The Writer's Guide: A companion to writing for pleasure or publication – Irina Dunn's 2002 guide for writers is an essential, comprehensive guide for both would-be and developing writers, from students to retirees, who are writing for publication or for pleasure.

Writing Down the Bones: Freeing the Writer Within – in this 1986 book, latest edition 2016, Natalie Goldberg suggests taking a Zen approach to writing by expanding on the concept of free writing to suggest what she calls writing practice. Like free writing, writing practice involves unstructured, uninhibited writing exercises, but is also about self-reflection.

The Elements of Style – this iconic book for writers, penned by William Strunk and E.B. White, was first published in 1918. The fourth edition, which appeared in 1999, continues to convey the principles of English style to its millions of readers. It provides students and writers with a blueprint that they can follow to write clearly and effectively while adhering to the rules of English grammar.

Writers' blogs

Anne Skyvington: The Craft of Writing
Creative writer Anne Skyvington blogs on the craft of writing and her life as a writer in Sydney, Australia. Her articles distil the research she does for her own creative writing and explore the fundamentals of writing and publishing. (http://anneskyvington.com.au/)

C.L. Larkin: Live Write Thrive
C.L. Larkin's blog covers a wide range of areas such as writing fundamentals, character emotion, reader empathy, becoming a masterful writer and grammar mistakes. At times she engages guest writers.

Critiquing and consultation services for writers, videos and online courses are also available. (https://www.livewritethrive.com/)

Dina Davis: Books and Writing
Author Dina Davis records advice and tips from other writers which she's learned along the way to publication, as well as her own personal experiences as a writer and writing group convenor. Her blog includes book reviews and some excerpts from her own works in progress. (http://dinadavisauthor.com)

Joanna Penn: The Creative Pen
Joanna is prolific and offers inspiration and information on writing, self-publishing and book marketing. She also offers a range of resources such as videos, books, courses and podcasts. She is a member of the Alliance of Independent Authors. (https://www.thecreativepenn.com/ blog/)

Acknowledgements

Randwick Writers' Group acknowledges the Gadigal people of the Eora nation and their elders past, present and emerging.

Sharing Writing Skills is a collaborative endeavour built on the work of past and present members of Randwick Writers' Group. Thank you particularly to the convenor, Dina Davis, for her initiative in suggesting this project; all authors and editors who contributed to the book; and Geraldine Star for her expertise in compiling the manuscript.

For their assistance, our appreciation also goes to
– author Thomas Keneally for his inspiring quotation
– members of Waverley Writers for helping to develop the works of some of the authors.

www.ingramcontent.com/pod-product-compliance
Lightning Source LLC
Chambersburg PA
CBHW062142100526
44589CB00014B/1666